RICH

BAXT

OF KIDDERMINSTER

& Flo, Thanks for all of your help. sincerely Nigel.

NIGEL KNOWLES

1st edition 300 copies

STAR AND GARTER PUBLISHERS
18 WELCH GATE
BEWDLEY
WORCS. DY12 2AT
Tel: 01299 402343

Printed by Stargold Ltd., Kidderminster

British Library Cataloguing-in-Publication Data. A Catalogue record for this book is available.

PUBLISHED 23rd NOVEMBER 2000
To coincide with a meeting of Kidderminster Charter Trustees

ISBN 0.9534704.0.7

STAR AND GARTER BOOKS

About The Author

Nigel Knowles was born in Worcester in 1946 and lived in Kidderminster until 1978 when he moved to Wood Green, London with his wife Jennifer, daughter Natasha and son Keiran. Nigel has pursued a number of occupations, including being a carpet weaver and a trade union education officer. He gained an Honours Degree in Politics and Certificate of Education. Nigel was five times a parliamentary candidate for the Labour Party and an elected Councillor in Haringey. He remains a Councillor in Bewdley and Kidderminster at Town, District and County level, and has also served as Chairman of Worcestershire County Council and Chairman of Wyre Forest District Council. This year Nigel is the Mayor of Kidderminster, and prospective Parliamentary Labour Candidate for Ludlow.

Photo by Valerie Grant

In 1990, Nigel was one of the Heinemann New Writers, with his comedy, "The Tailors Dummy."

Other books by Nigel Knowles, still available from 'Star and Garter,' are:

"Those in Favour." ISBN . 0. 9519130. 0.X. Price £5.00

"Observations Inside a Bewdley Ice-Cream Parlour."
ISBN.09519130.18. Price £4.00

"Identity Crisis." ISBN.0.9519130.2.C. Price £4.00

"Lord Lucan - The Letters of Sabrina." (*Out of Print*)
ISBN.0.9519130.3.4. Price £5.00

"Politics, Sex and Garlic Mushrooms." ISBN.0.9519130.4.2. £4.99

"Bewdley 1762 - The Diary of Jack Nowles" ISBN.09519130.50. Price £4.00

"Bewdley Parish Magazine 1886." ISBN.09519130.69. Price £6.99

"American Revolution 1776 - Letters from New York, Boston and London"
ISBN.09519130.77. Price £10.00

"Bewdley Parish Magazine 1878-1880" ISBN.09519130.8.5. Price £10.00

"De Gaulle and the Free French in Bewdley 1942-1944"
ISBN.09519130.93. Price £12.00

RICHARD BAXTER OF KIDDERMINSTER

Nigel Knowles

CONTENTS

Note

All photographs were taken by Nigel Knowles during the summer of 2000 and the front cover Baxter print is his.

Richard Baxter and Kidderminster

FOREWORD

During his trial at Westminster hall in 1685 the infamous Judge Jeffreys said of Richard Baxter,
"This is an old rogue, and hath poisoned the world with his Kidderminster doctrine he deserves to be whipped through the city". Baxter was imprisoned but thankfully spared the whipping. But Richard Baxter is forever associated with Kidderminster. His time as preacher at Kidderminster Parish Church of St.Marys and All Saints is considered to have been his most fruitful and important. His tenure coincided with the Civil War, surely England's most turbulent and violent period of political and civic conflict.
I have reprinted two important articles herein about Richard Baxter and his time in Kidderminster. They were written in 1923 by Thomas Cave, a member of the Worcestershire Historical Society.

THE FIRST ESSAY

Thomas Cave considers evidence concerning seating and galleries in St. Mary's Church Kidderminster at the time of Richard Baxter. The debate centres around the issues of permission, authority and reasons for installing the seating. Were pews and galleries put in to accommodate new members of the church who were recruited by Baxter? Were galleries erected to replace lost or broken seating, "during the late unhappy time," or was the issue primarily about Lord Windsor's request for a family gallery?
Cave takes issue with Mathew Sylvester's assertion in his 1696, "Narrative of the life and times of Richard Baxter," Quote, "That during his Ministry at Kidderminster, we were fain to build five galleries after my coming thither". Cave claims the statement to be misleading.

THE SECOND ESSAY

Thomas Cave gives an account of Baxter's life taken from Mathew Sylvester's, "Narrative of the life and times of Richard Baxter",(Edition 1696), which was, quote, "Chiefly Baxter's own words, given in his Life by his friend Mr Mathew Sylvester".

RICHARD BAXTER
1615 - 1691

The following notes give a local, national and international perspective to the life of Richard Baxter. I strongly believe such a perspective is essential in understanding his life and work.

The religious and political turmoil and upheaval which occurred during the 17th century was not peculiar to England. Indeed the split within the Christian church resulting in the formation of the Protestant movement away from Catholicism had its' roots equally in Europe, as in England.

There was the further clash, medieval in fact, between the Christian and other faiths, particularly Muslim. Very brief reference is made in the Chronology of important dates to the Turks (Muslim) being expelled from parts of Europe during Baxter's time. The antecedents of that of course were the mortally violent Christian Crusades against the Muslim powers of the East. The legacy remained until the Turks and Muslims were expelled from Spain and Europe in the 17th Century.

There was and is, therefore a world which is outside both England and Baxter's own habitats in Shropshire, Worcestershire, London and elsewhere. That world needs to be at least hinted at in this paper. It is only by comparison with other men and women,and the events of the world, that we are able to judge the impact and influence of Richard Baxter. We need to make reference to his religion and the religion of others; the political and military events; the cultural, artistic, musical, poetic and literary contributions. This, I have tried to do, albeit briefly.

I believe 17th century questions of religious tolerance have to be judged against the terrible persecutions which had occurred in the centuries before, and indeed were still occurring. The colonisation of North America was directly related to religious persecution and intolerance. In England these questions also took on the specific political demands of a rising class of bourgeois merchants and entrepaneurs. This movement led to the execution of King Charles 1st.

Baxter seems not to have been a radical exponent of political change, more seemingly an advocate of Puritanism against the then dominant Protestant church of England, with the particular commitment to a new religious order which was non-Catholic and tolerant of evangelical churches, allowing new forms of religious practice, worship and teaching. This Puritan or Presbyterian form was to be non-corrupted and set within a framework of toleration and religious freedom of expression.

Baxter himself claims to have preferred the option of remaining neutral on the issue of Parliament versus Monarchy, instead of having to side with Parliament. But his choice for Parliament was quickly rescinded at the Restoration of 1660 when he became Chaplain to Charles 2nd. The charge of political expediency might be levelled against Baxter, because he had held a chaplaincy position in Cromwell's army also. Baxter was a political survivor.

But his persecution, particularly under the Stuarts probably only confirmed his prejudice against Political Monarchs and Political Parliamentarians engaging in religious and other mortal disputes. Baxter therefore could be seen as a religious exponent caught up in deadly political turmoil. He was not party political. Yet the religious conflict abounding in England during his time meant that his actions and his writings were considered a political threat. This was because his Puritanism went against the status quo, his refusal to comply with Church of England edicts resulted in his, and many others, being placed outside the relative safety of the established church.

The result of 17th century religious and political strife remains with us as tangible evidence - the Monarchy has its place within the Constitution, recognising the supremacy of Parliament. A living vestige remains in the fact that a Catholic still may not inherit the throne, or indeed the Monarch be married to a Catholic.

The Protestant religion is the dominant religion in Britain, toleration of other religions and faiths being implicitly acknowledged both within the Protestant faith and Government legislation.

Consideration of Richard Baxter's life and work should indeed throw light on the social, religious and political circumstances of 17th century England. There is enough evidence to suggest that Baxter was an important figure who took part in the great events of his age - The English Civil War and the turbulence within the religious order.

His contribution should be seen in those terms. There were Englishmen of greater or of equally great importance - Milton, Locke, Hobbes,Shakespeare, Pepys, Bunyan, Purcell, Newton.

Yet Richard Baxter has an important place within English history as a Reforming Pastor of National consequence. His, "The Saints' Everlasting Rest," is known throughout the world, as is his association with Kidderminster and its parish church of St. Mary's. I hope that my publication of this work helps to allow further consideration and appreciation of Richard Baxter and the issues of political and religious tolerance.

We return to the life of Richard Baxter. The preceding pages demonstrate the turbulence and violence of his period, one irony being that Baxter's life ended as the Disputation about Parliament and Monarchy was itself drawing to a close - each would live in peace with the other. But religious tolerance was not achieved; Catholics being persecuted as a state article of faith.

According to contemporary observers and friends, Richard Baxter was not at all a robust man who enjoyed the best of health. Indeed, he is herein described as (sic), a weakly person, subject to frequent illness ... with a troubled, sad disposition.

However, it is relevant to note various other considerations concerning Baxter's health and disposition. Firstly, he survived the appalling and dangerous blood-letting practice of the time when he suffered serious illnesses. Secondly although apparently not of a vigorous constitution, at 46 years of age Baxter married Margaret Charlton who was just 22 years old. It could be concluded therefore, that Baxter was well enough for marriage, even if Margaret saw him as a rather saintly or unworldly man with a national reputation and committed to religious worship and study, rather than expecting a normal physical married life. Indeed, Margaret was to die first on 14th June, 1681 in her 41st year.

Thirdly, Baxter survived politically and physically, throughout England's most turbulent internal period, surviving imprisonment and persecution under Kings and Lord Protector, outliving his "persecutor in chief," Judge Jeffreys, who himself was to die in prison. And fourth, Baxter lived until he was aged 76, dying peacefully at home. Not many could equal that, who lived then.

Psychologically perhaps, Baxter's apparent physical weakness was a strength because his disposition presented opportunity, maybe the necessity, to write his religious works. He expected to be called to his Everlasting Rest on many occasions, always considering his current work to likely be his last. But conversely his assured likelihood of early death compelled Baxter to, (sic)" be strong for God," to serve and to write as many manuscripts as possible whilst he was physically able.

NOTES ON KIDDERMINSTER AND BEWDLEY DURING BAXTERS TIME AND THE CIVIL WAR PERIOD

KIDDERMINSTER

YEAR		POPULATION
1608	-	1,500
1647	-	2,200
1685	-	3,000

OCCUPATIONS
Between 1540 and 1655.

Weaving, fulling, cloth working and milling, shoe making, haberdashery, saddling, sawyers, wire drawers, cutlers, mercers, dyers, shermen, tailors, arrow makers, barbers, surgeons, tanners, glovers, cappers, bakers, millwrights, butchers, curriers, mountebanks, bellmen, doctors, apothecaries, schoolmasters, deacons, squires, soldiers, ragmen, grinders, papermakers, a jockey, a singer, a freemason, a vicar, a minister, a knight and their servants.

TAX

Sheriff's figures for the levy of Ship Money 1635
Assessment for Worcestershire was £4,000.
Worcester City assessed £266, Evesham £84, Bewdley £70, Kidderminster £30 and the clergy £1,118. Remainder from districts.

CHARTER

Kidderminster's Charter was granted in 1636 by King Charles I. It is 52 pages long and creates one corporate body, to remain the free borough corporate of the Bailiff and Burgesses of Kidderminster. The first High Steward was Sir Ralph Clare. There was one High Bailiff and 12 capital burgesses who formed the common council of the Borough, to make such laws as necessary, to levy money for repair of bridges, streets, paths etc., to hold markets and punish offenders. Constables and Justices of the Peace were appointed. 25 citizens were to be Chief Burgesses to support the High Bailiff, elections were annual.

THE GRAMMAR SCHOOL

The Kidderminster Grammar School dates from 1566. The Charter of 1636 allowed K.G.S. to be known as King Charles 1st Grammar School.

BEWDLEY

During the 17th century, Bewdley was an important centre of commerce and river trading.

YEAR	POPULATION	YEAR	POPULATION	YEAR	POPULATION
1600	= 1,800	1640	= 3,000	1691	= 2,800
1621	= 1,800	1661	= 2,900	1700	= 2,800

Bewdley had many of the trades found also in Kidderminster. Of equal importance was the political and religious nature of Bewdley, particularly so because of the proximity of each town to the other - a mere three miles.

It is evident from parish records that Puritans, Baptists, Quakers and Presbyterians were to be found in Bewdley during Baxter's time, and a number held prominent positions in the social order, being of the artisan and entrepeneur class, as well as being evident within the ranks of Bewdley town burgesses. Two dozen were removed from their posts after the Restoration of Charles II for their refusal to take the oath regarding the Solemn League and Covenant incorporated into the 1661 Corporation Act (England and Scotland agreed help from Scots army in return for a religious settlement on a reformed model, giving apparent freedom for Presbyterianism in England and Scotland - sent 1643. Therefore, the Royalist-Parliament, Anglican-Nonconformist was very evident in Bewdley during Baxter's time. Indeed, Baxter was a particular friend of Robert Morton, who between 1635 and 1646, was the Curate of Bewdley Chapel. He was followed by John Tombes the Anabaptist Curate, 1646 to 1650. Bewdley Baptists owed their origin to him. (Founder of Bewdley's Puritans Gilbert - page 13.)

The next incumbent was Henry Oasland MA., another friend and ally of Richard Baxter. At this time, the Rector of Ribbesford was John Boraston MA., a Royalist who supported Sir Ralph Clare of Kidderminster, a strong opponent of Baxter. The Quakers were also evident in Bewdley, meeting at the house of Jacob Cotterell, a currier.

In 1999, I published, "Bewdley Parish Magazine 1878 and 1880", reproduced verbatim from the original. The 1878 version gives a very important contemporary account of the life and work of the Reverend Henry Oasland, Minister of St. Anne's, Bewdley, (1650-1662). The account is in two parts, the first being autobiographical, and the second by his son, the Reverend Edward Oasland, Pastor of the old Presbyterian Chapel in Bewdley High Street. The 1880 Bewdley Parish Magazine gives an equally valuable account of Rev. John Boraston MA.

Boraston held his church position in Ribbesford for 58 years from 1630 until 1688. He came under great pressure from the Puritans who tried, unsuccesfully, to have him removed from office. The article was written for the Bewdley Parish Magazine 1878 by J.R. Burton

Note: James II gave Bewdley a new Charter in 1685, replacing the Charter of 1605, which incorporated Bewdley's Free Grammar School.

KING CHARLES I GRAMMAR SCHOOL KIDDERMINSTER AND BAXTER

During Baxter's time in Kidderminster, the Grammar School was situated in the Chantry of St. Mary's Church. There is no evidence that Baxter taught therein, but records indicate he was involved in supporting the interests of pupils.
In his book, "King Charles I Grammar School," Don Gilbert cites 1566 as the year when a, "Free Grammar School", was founded. Documents discovered at Ivens and Morton's solicitors in 1949 by Michael James and A.J. Perrett, contemporary History Master (who incidentallly taught me between 1957 and 1962), indicate Sir Edward Blount gave lands to the school governors (Feoffees), stating the Grammar School had been founded by his father Thomas. A free school had been created in 1550.
The Kidderminster Charter of Incorporation of 1636 granted various trading rights, fairs and markets to the Borough and included a section on the school, (in Latin), ..."there shall be one Grammar School which shall be called the free Grammar School of Charles, King of England, in Kidderminster."

THE CIVIL WAR AROUND KIDDERMINSTER AND BEWDLEY

The area was not one in which nationally significant events occured during the English Civil War - there were no major battles, such as occurred at Worcester, rather the peripheral skirmishes, retreats and movements associated with conflict elsewhere throughout the country.

However, like everywhere else in England, the people of Kidderminster and Bewdley were subject to the violence and turmoil endemic in the war. The towns were not burned down, there were no seiges and few actual contests between the military representatives of Parliament and the Monarchy. But, soldiers were killed in the vicinity, at Kidderminster, for instance, near to St. Mary's church and at Trimpley 1645-46. A Royalist force was defeated at Trimpley on 8 November 1645 and in December, Kidderminster was plundered by Royalist Cavalry.

In 1642, Parliamentary forces under Lords Brooke and Wharton were sent to Kidderminster, to intercept Prince Rupert en-route to London. Wharton retreated, abandoning wagons and military equipment which were given over to the Royalists by Kidderminster people.

In 1644 General Waller entered Kidderminster with Parliamentary forces, declaring it "little better than an empty farm". In 1645, after the Battle of Naseby, King Charles I came through Kidderminster on 1st July, enroute to Bewdley.

Bewdley saw some military action. King Charles I had Quarters in the town at Tickenhill Palace on 12th June 1644, staying for 3 nights, escaping from General Waller (based at Kidderminster) by boat down the Severn to Worcester. The King returned to Bewdley again a year later, staying at The Angel Hotel on 17th June 1645 after his disasterous battle of Naseby.

Sir Thomas Lyttleton, the Govenor of Bewdley was based at Tickenhill Palace in May 1644. The Parliamentary Colonel John "Tinker" Fox led a force across Bewdley bridge, tricking the Royalist guards by impersonating a Royalist troop, took Tickenhill and held Lyttelton.

The townsfolk of Kidderminster and Bewdley were in some dread of looting and worse from opposing Royalist and Parliamentary forces. For whatever reason, possibly because Bewdley fell to the Parliamentarians, the Bewdley Bailiff, was executed by order of the King.

The Scots defeated a Royalist force under Richard Lord Molyneux at Bewdley on 13 August 1645, taking 70 prisoners and killing three, who were buried at Ribbesford.

And so, the major events of the Civil War 1642-1651 occurred elsewhere. But King Charles I was present on several occasions in the Kidderminster and Bewdley vicinity, albeit fleeing for his life at one time. Richard Baxter was lucky to survive; indeed for some 5 years he took refuge away from Kidderminster, ensuring his safety under the protection of Parliament in Coventry and other places.

THE ENGLISH CIVIL WAR

The English Civil War 1642 - 1649 is argued by some to have been a class issue. The new rising class of entrepreneur - merchants were considered to have asserted their political and commercial rights at the mortal expense of King Charles 1st and his old ruling-class bourgeois landed aristocrats. For others, emphasis would be placed upon religious conflict; Catholicism versus the Anglican Church of England with the Monarchy seeking to restore wealth and privilege both to itself and the Catholic Church at the expense of Parliament, the Church of England and its various constituent parts which were Puritan, Presbyterian, Baptist, Quaker etc.

It is likely that a combination of such issues caused the Civil War, with the ordinary people being equally divided between King and Parliament. The result however is not at issue. King Charles 1st was executed on 30th January, 1649 and in 1653 Oliver Cromwell was installed as Lord Protector in a Parliament which he controlled until his death on 3rd September, 1658.

The political issue of Monarchy versus Parliament was not settled for another 30 years, continuing through Richard Cromwell's Protectorate of 1658-1659, (he retired and died peacefully in 1712). The apparent victory of the Monarchy in 1660 upon the Restoration of King Charles 2nd was not complete, though at that time it must have seemed so. Oliver Cromwell's body was disinterred then hanged on a gallows at Tyburn on 30 January 1661 (the 12th anniversary of Charles 1st's execution). Cromwell's head was placed on a pole in Westminster Hall and the trunk buried beneath the gallows.

Charles 2nd ruled between 1660 and 1685, but his period was a turbulent one in which his preference for the Catholic Church and absolute "Kingly power," caused continual challenge and unrest. Indeed, on his death bed 6th February, 1685, Charles 2nd was received into the Catholic Church. His legacy therefore was to give credance to his successor, the Catholic James 2nd, who began to victimise and persecute Dissenters and Puritans, Baxter included.

But James 2nd did not have sufficiently powerful support from the Grandees and Parliamentarians of the day. His reign lasted only 3 years between 1685 and 1688, when he effectively abdicated by fleeing the country to France.

The "Bloodless Revolution" saw the installation of William 3rd of Orange. His wife was Mary, daughter of James 2nd.

But the right to inherit the Monarchy was still challenged. In England and in Holland, plans were made for a rising led by the Duke of Monmouth, one of the illegitimate offsprings of Charles 2nd. In June 1688, Monmouth landed in Lyme Regis with thousands of men and was welcomed by the labourers, small holders and weavers. His banner was the old one of Leveller green. But none of the great Whig Lords gave him support, and few of the gentry.

Monmouth's army was beaten at Sedgemoor in a bloody battle in which Monmouth's untrained army of peasants and weavers were slaughtered by the Government's disciplined troops and cavalry. Survivors were tried at "The Bloody Assizes" by Judge Jeffreys; hundreds were executed including Monmouth and hundreds were transported to the West Indies as virtual slaves for the plantations. The beneficiary of the "Bloodless Revolution" was William.

Negotiations were opened on 30th June between the Whigs and Tories (Government) and William of Orange. William landed unopposed at Torbay on 5th November 1688. In February 1689 a Convention offered the throne to William and Mary. The Convention declared itself a Parliament and also instigated The Bill of Rights. The King would no longer control the army or judiciary and Parliament gained control of finance. Parliament would be called at least once in every three years, and could only last for that same period.

According to A. L. Morton in his, "A Peoples' History of England," and quoting Karl Marx, - "this Glorious Revolution, brought into power, along with William of Orange, the landlord and capitalist appropriators of surplus value. They inaugurated the new era by practising on a colossal scale, thefts of State lands. These estates were given away without legal etiquette. The Crown Lands thus fraudently appropriated, together with the Church estates ....form the basis of the today princely domains of the English Oligarchy. The bourgeois capitalists favoured the operation, to promote free trade, extend the domain of modern agriculture on the large farm system, and to increase their supply of agricultural proletarians."

In 1689 James 2nd landed in Ireland where he gained support from his Catholic army. In July 1690, William defeated the Jacobite army at the Battle of the Boyne. William promised religious tolerance for Irish Catholics, but promptly broke it by severe Penal Laws depriving Catholics of all civil and religious rights. Oppression followed throughout Ireland, lands were confiscated and the rule was brutal.

William was accepted in Scotland, after the rising at Killiecrankie. By 1692, William was undisputed throughout the British Isles.

ESSAY ONE

THOMAS CAVE - THE GALLERIES AND PEWS OF ST. MARY'S AROUND BAXTER'S TENURE THERIN.

To The Reader.

A FORMER, and very limited edition having been issued of the aforegiven Articles, viz. : " John Baskervile (1706-1775) The Printer : his ancestry " and " Richard Baxter and Kidderminster Parish Church," and which met with general approval. Its re-issue, at the request of a few friends, together with a brief account of the Life and Ministry of Richard Baxter (1615-1662), and such historical incidents of that period relative to the Town and Parish of Kidderminster in general would be acceptable, as to need no apology for the comments on Baxter, they being given in the light and spirit of modern thought. His marble figure adorns the centre of the Town, as if with uplifted hand, in act of exhortation, bidding all to be of good cheer, it adds dignity to the chief scene of his labours, and in the background that Church bearing his name, claiming to be his spiritual descendent.

THOMAS CAVE

RICHARD BAXTER,

AND

KIDDERMINSTER.

PART I.

CERTAIN Documents, in the Bishop's Registry, Worcester, appearing at variance with the statement in Mr. Mathew Sylvester's, " Narrative of the Life and Times of Richard Baxter, p 84, Ed. 1696." That is, " That during his Ministry at Kidderminster, we were fain to build five galleries after my coming thither." A statement explicit, and followed by all writers, but misleading, hitherto a stumbling block, to an observant person, as to the manner, and form.

Prior to Baxter's ministry there is reason to believe, that the only gallery, if such did then exist, would be the Road loft, at the division of the chancel, from the Nave, and that the sittings were on the ground floor, much damaged during the " late Unhappy time," allotted, and annexed to some house in the parish as shown hereinafter. The Parish Register (1620) shows an Order, That by the consent of the Vicar and Churchwardens that nine newly enlarged seats were allowed to be made, and maintained by certain parishoners, at their own cost, and amounting to 40 shillings, or thereabout, next unto the middle alley in the said Church.

Baxter tells the Church was usually so full, that it was necessary to build the said Galleries.

What is generally understood in the ordinary acceptation of the statement? Were they galleries running longitudinally, an upper, and a lower tier along the North, and South Arcades, and one other usually at the West end, or in what form, and manner understood by the general reader? A professional Journal (Building News, July 31, 1914) says such galleries were impracticable owing to the low pitch of the roof of the Nave Arcades, and to which an intelligent observer, will be in agreement.

How then, are we to understand such statement, but in the conclusion arrived at after examination of the following Documents Nos. 2509, 2510, 2513, 7093, 7078, 7707, 7747, 7748 in said Registry. Nos. 2509-10 show a Gallery erected in the Church, without Legal Authority, during the "late Unhappy times" by which is understood, the Interregnum period, situated in the South Eastern arcade of the Church, about five yards in length, extending from pillar to pillar, and having a passage leading up to it, under one of the Southern Arcade windows that stand behind the said Eastern part of the said Gallery, and conclusively show it as being a row of five parallel sittings in the S.E. arcade of the said Church.

Prior to Baxter's departure from the Town (1662) The Restoration Government had appointed Lord Windsor as Lord Lieutenant of the County, and he chosen a House in Kidderminster for residence, and it was in right of his house, this faculty 2509 was granted of a sitting for himself, Lady, and family. A Capital, or Mansion House, usually had a right to a sitting for the said house to those dwelling thereof, wherein to sit, and hear Divine Worship in their Parish Church.

Prior to Baxter going away, he asked Lord Windsor to intervene in any strife, or misrepresentation, against his old flock, their sole desire being to live in peace with all men.

N°. 2509.

Timothy Baldwyn, Doctor of Laws to the Right Reverend Father in Christ, William by divine permission Lord Bishop of Worcester, etc. To the Vicar, or Curate of the Parish Church of Kidderminster, Dioc. of Worc$^{r.}$ Greeting, Whereas it is made appear to me Timothy Baldwyn, Chancellor of the Diocese of Worcester, by the Right Honorable, Thomas, Lord Windsor, Lord Lieutenant of his Majesties Forces, within the County of Worcester, That he having a Mansion House in the sayd parish of Kidderminster, wherein, himselfe, with his Lady, children, and family doe now inhabit, and noe convenient seat in the sayd Church, for them to heare Divine Service, and whereas there is a gallery erected in the late Unhappy time on the South side of the sayd Church without my lawfull authority, And the seates thereon fixed, not appropriated to the responsible persons nowe sittinge there by my lawfull authority, whereby some debate and disturbance may in future time arise concerning the propriety thereof. These we therefore require you the sayd Vicar, or Curate, That upon the next Lord's day after the reception hereof, you give publick notice in the sayd Church of Kidderminster, That I doe intend to appropriate to the sayd Right Honorable, Thomas, Lord Windsor a part of the sayd South Gallery, being Five yards in length at the Eastern end thereof, extending itselfe from Pillar, to Pillar, together with a passage up to it, to be made under one of the Southern windows, that stand behind the sayd Eastern pte of the sayd Gallery, for the sayd Lord Windsor, his Lady, and Family to heare Divine service, And that you further publish in the sayd Church unto the psons that ptend Interest in the sayd Gallery. That they appeare before me, or my lawful Surrogate in the Consistory Court place in the Cathedral Church of Worcester, upon Thursday, the Fifftenth day of this instant Feb$^{y.}$ betwixt the houres of nine and twelve in the morning, then, and there to showe cause, if they have any, why the sayd pte of the sayd Gallery may not be assigned, and appropriated unto the sayd Lord Windsor, as aforesaid, or otherwise, I doe intend to proceed, and will proceede to the appropriation of the same as aforesayd, according to the Lawes, and that you further intimate to the sayd parishioners, That I doe hereby give Liberty, for the buildinge, and erectinge of an additional pte unto the Gallery on the North side of the sayd Church to continue in Length three yards, and three quarters, and in breadth two yards, and a half, for the placing of those persons who are nowe to be removed accordinge to my order in that behalf.

Given at Worcester, under the Seal of our office, on the first day of the month of February, In the year of our Lord, according to the Computation of England 1665.

This was done, as ordered, on the 4th day of Feby in the parish Church of Kidderminster 1665.

Geo Dance, Vicar.

N$^{o.}$ 2510. The concluding part of each line is decayed, as shown by *Italics* but can be inferred by aforegiven N$^{o.}$

Feby 12th 1665.

It is agreed betweene the Right Hon$^{ble.}$ Thomas Lord windesor *and the Inhabitants* of the Towne of Kidderminster, that have for some *years been sitting* in a certaine Gallery, standinge on the South side of the Church, *concerning which* was an order directed to the Vicar of Kidderminster from the *worshipful Timothy* Baldwyn, Dr. of Laws, and Chancellor of the See of Worcester *and hereby* publish his designs of appropriating to the said Lord Windesor, *part of the South* Gallery, lying on the East end thereof, extending it to sette from *Pillar to Pillar*, five yards in length, together that there should be an addition to the *North Gallery*, at the expense, and charges of the said Lord windesor for the seating *of those persons* removed out of the former, the said Lord windesor, is contented and *each hereby*, are agreed, that there shall be halfe of those foure first seates *in the East* Gallery being equally divided, and all the upper part, or east end *appropriated* to Lord windesor, and his heirs, and the other part thereof to be *confirmed to the use of the* Inhabitants, and their heires for ever, and that if the Loft, or Gallery, *connected*, by an inscription of its being at the Disposall of the Minister for *continuance be hereby*, confirmed to them, the Lord windesor shall not be putt to adde to the *costs and charges*, but the confirmation of it, to them, and their heires, that is to say *Those persons* as shall be removed and have subscribed to this paper, with a full satisfaction to them. In witness, *whereof we have* subscribed our names—

Thomas Taylor	Robert Cooper	2nd Column
William pitt	Richard Warham	
Richard Clarke	Ed Thomas	
Thomas Reade	Thomas Bellamy	
William Reade	Richard heminge Junr.	
Joshua Malpas	Will haywood	3rd Column
William Mumford	William bourne	
Lawrence Pearsall	William bourne	
Richard Hemming	Thomas Potter	
Edmund Reade	John Brettle	
	John Browne	

There were a 4th row of signatures, but lost as in manner stated, by decay.

It would appear by the following Mandate No. 2513 that certain persons did persist in sitting in said South Gallery, other than those whose names are above given.

" Timothy Baldwyn, Dcor of Laws, and Chancellor of the Reverend Father in God, Robert by divine permission, Lord Bishop of the Diocesse of Worcester, To our beloved in Christ Mr. George Dance, Clerke, Vicar of the parish Church of Kidderminster, in the Diocesse of Worcr. aforesayd or his Curate there, Greeting, Whereas it is manifested unto us that of your parish doe sitt in a Gallery, erected in ye late unhappy tymes in the sayd Church of Kidderminster, whereon is written (To bee at ye Disposalle of the Minister) without any lawfull Authortie. Wee doe therefore will, and by these presents require you the sayd Vicar or Curate, that upon the next Sunday, or Holy day after the receipt hereof, in ye Church of Kidderminster aforesayd, you Inhibit the sayde persons from further presuming, or attempting to sitt in, or possess themselves of any part of the sayd Gallery, duringe the tyme of divine service, or sermons (it beinge already assigned, and allotted by us, for other persons) unless they appear before us, or our lawfull Surrogate in the Consistory Court place in ye Cathedral Church of Worcr. upon Thursday, the 15th day of this instant, March, betweene the howers of 9 and 12 of the Clocke, in the fournoon of the same day then, and there, to show lawfull, and reasonable changes to the contrary, and that you further Warne the sayd persons, that in case they do not appear accordinglie they doe hereafter desist from cominge, or intrudinge into the sayd Gallerie, and doe suffer, and permit the same to bee peaceably, and quietly enjoyed, and possessed by those persons for whom it is appointed, and assigned, upon pain of the Law, and Contempt. And what you do in the premises, you are to certify us, or our Surrogate, upon sayd howers, and place. Given at Worcester under the Seale of our office, the 2nd day of March, in the year of our Lord (Accordinge to the Computation of the Church of England) 1665.

Tho Vernon, Register

The aforegiven Nos. 2509—10—13 have reference to the said Gallery, erected during the Ministry of Baxter. Its further allottment and additions in lieu of desturbance.

The following Documents have no reference to Baxter ministry, but given in support that continuous galleries were not intended by Baxter statement. Additions being made at varied periods to meet the need of a growing populations in the parish.

No. 7077 mandate in answer to a petition, issued by order of Timothy Baldwyn D.L. etc. to the Rector, Vicar, or Curate of the Parish Church of Kidderminster.

Whereas, the Minister, Churchwardens, and some others of the parishioners of Kidderminster, in the County, and Diocese of Worcester, have presented a Petition unto their Ordinary, thereby showing that severall of the Inhabitants of the said parish, doe want convenient places in the said parish Church of Kidderminster, to sit, and kneele in to hear Divine Service and Sermon, and thereby have prayed Licence to erect a Gallery in a vacant place, on the North side of the said Church containinge sixteene foot in length, and eleaven feet in breadth, for the parishoners there to sit, and kneele to hear Divine Service, and Sermon, It being a very convenient place for that purpose I doe therefore by virtue of this mandate to me directed. Cite peremplorily all, and every person, and persons claiminge and pretendinge to any Right, title, or interest in, or to the said vacant place, they, or every of them doe appear before the Right Worshipfull, Sir Timothy Baldwyn, Kn$^{t.}$ Doct. of Law and Chancellor of the Diocese of Worcester, or his lawfull Surrogate in the Cathedral Church of Worcester (at the time etc. cited)

Sealed 16th September 1680. Thos. Vernon, Reg$^{r.}$

All manner of persons, that can, or will object, why ?

Execu—Rad Clare Mil et M$^{r.}$ Toye

N$^{o.}$ 7093, which is undated, is evidently the Petition To Sir Timothy Baldwin, Knight, and Bishop's Chancellor of the Diocese of Worcester.

Wee whose names are hereunto subscribed being the Vicar and Churchwardens of Kidderminster, in the county of Worc$^{r.}$ doe hereby certifie y^{r} Wor^{p} that by Reason that severall of the Inhabitants of this Burrough doe want places in the Church, That wee doe think it convenient that there be a new Loft erected in the Church, that soe those that want, may be supplied, and wee intreate yo$^{r.}$ Worshipp to grant Licence to John Lynall to erect, and build a new Loft on the North side of the Church which may containe 16 foote in Length, and 11 foote in Breadth, which wee finde to be a convenient place, and will not in any way be pjudishall to any person, as is hereunto subscribed by

Richard White, Vicar.
John woodward }
Nicholas Radford } Churchwardens.
Francis F Haycox
his mark.

The dimensions here given are approximate to a Side Nave Arcade of Kidderminster Parish Church.

No. 7078 is given as a proof, that the accommodation for worship in the Parish Church was much destroyed during the Civil War, while in the hands of the rival parties. It is a Mandate by Sir Timothy Baldwyn Kt. Dr. of Law, and Bishop's Chancellor of the Diocese of Worcester, to the Rector, Vicar, or Curate of the Parish Church of Kidderminster that on the next Sunday, or festival following after the date, and receiving of this order, that during the time of Divine Service he shall read out, declare to the whole Congregation, the following command in the English tongue.

Whereas Capel Hanbury Esqe. of this parish is Destitute of a Convenient seat, place, or Pew, to sit, and kneele in Duringe the Time of Divine Service, and Sermon, and hath shewed unto the Ordinary, that there is a convenient place where his Father's pew was before the War, about five foot in length, and six foot in breadth within the Church of Kidderminster, under the longe Gallery, where Mr. Foley sits, the seat of one John Wall, being on the East side, the seat wherein the wife of william . . . . being on the West side, and ye upper end of the seates, called the (Gallery) seates, on the North side, which he hath prayed may be assigned, and allotted to him, to erect a convenient, and decent seat, or pew thereupon for himselfe, and family, to sit, and kneele to hear Divine Service, and Sermon, I doe therefore by virtue to me directed, Cite peremporily, all, and every person, or persons claiminge, and pretending any Right, title, or Interest in, or to the said place, or ground, that they, and every of them doe appear before the Right Worshipfull, Sir Timothy Baldwyn, Knight, Dr. of Laws and Chancellor of the Diocese of Worcester, or his lawfull Surrogate in the Cathedral Church of Worc$^{r.}$ and in the Consistory place there on Thursday, the last of this instant September, between the hours of nine and twelve of the Clock, in the forenoon of the same day, to show sufficient and reasonable causes if they can, why the said place, or ground, ought not to be assigned, and allotted unto the said Capel Hanbury, Esq$^{e.}$ for the erectinge of a seat, or Pew thereupon, for his use, and his family, and further to doe, and receive as the Law shall require, And I intimate unto all, and every such person, or persons claiminge, or pretending, that if they doe not appear, and show cause, the assigning, and allotting of the place, or ground to the said Capel Hanbury Esq$^{e.}$ for the uses above-mentioned, their absence, or continuary in nowice notwithstanding.

Given under the seal of our office 23 September 1680.
Tho Vernon Reg^{r}

The Capel Hanbury above mentioned claimed in right of his house at Horestone, and was a person of some weight and influence in the County of Worcester, evidenced by the Sudsidy Papers (in the parish Chest) of assessments made and presented to their majesties (William III. and Mary) Commissioners, according to Act of Parliament. For many years, he appears as a Commissioner for Taxation.

He may be said, to be the originator of the immense wealth of his successors, the Hanbury Tracy line, at Pontypool, County of Monmouth. He himself was buried in the Chancel of Kidderminster Parish Church, 170$\frac{4}{5}$, January 20$^{h.}$

It appears also from the following documents N$^{os.}$ 7747—7748, That there was still a demand for seating in the Parish Church, whether it was by piety, force of Law, or increase of population, the demand was made.

7747. Timothy Baldwyn, K$^{t.}$ and D$^{r.}$ of Laws, etc. issued the Mandate, to our beloved in Christ, the Rector, Vicar, or Curate of the Parish Church of Kidderminster, to be read out to the congregation assembled during Divine

Service, the next Lord's day, or nearest festival, immediately after the Date and receipt thereof in the English tongue, the following words, viz.: Whereas ye Churchwardens of ye parish Church of Kidderminster, in ye County, and Diocese of Worcester, have petitioned their Ordinary, for leave to erect a Gallery in ye upper end of ye church upon ye Front of ye Scholars Gallery 29 foot in length, and five foot in breadth for ye convenience of ye parishoners. I doe therefore by virtue of this mandate to me directed, cite all manner of persons, that can show any just cause why Licence should not be granted to ye said Churchwardens, for ye erecting of the said Gallery that they appear if they think fit, in ye Cathedral Church of Worcester, and in ye Consistory place thereon Thursday ye fifteenth day of March, instant, between ye hours of nine and twelve, of ye Clocke, in ye forenoon of ye same day before ye Judge of ye said Court, then, and there to propound their objections in due form of Law, and further to doe, and receive as ye Law shall require. Intimating to all such persons, that if they doe not appear accordingly, or if they doe appear, and show not a just cause to ye contrary, ye Judge of ye said Court will proceed to grant Licence to y^{e} Churchwardens for y^{e} erecting of y^{e} said Gallery, (the absence, or rather continuary of all persons soe cited in any wise nothwithstanding).

Given under the seal of our Office, the day of March (. . .) in the year of our Lord, English style 1682.

Tho Vernon Reg$^{r.}$

It was read out on Lord's day, March 4th 168$\frac{2}{3}$

Rich$^{d.}$ Whi(te). Kedarm$^{sr.}$

N$^{o.}$ 7748. The several upper lines of this Document are wholly destroyed and can be inferred by the foregiven mandates, part legible being, viz. :

" they should appeare (. . .) propound their objection in due form of Law, one M$^{r.}$ Richard (. . .) Dobbins Impropriator of y^{e} Tythes of Kidderminster, aforesaid, hath by his Proctor appeared before our Surrogate, and alledged that y^{e} erecting of y^{e} said Gallery will be very prejudicall to y^{e} Chancell of y^{e} said Church in several respects viz : That it will *not* quite seperate ye body of ye Church, from ye Chancell, and hinder ye light of ye Chancell, and that ye persons sitting in ye said Chancell will not be able to heare Ministers voice in case ye said Gallery be erected as is above described, whereupon a Commission to view, and inspect ye same hath bin prayed by ye said parties. Wee therefore by these psents doe constitute you (in whose fidelity wee doe much confide) Commissioners to view and inspect ye same, giving, and by these presents grantinge unto you full power, and authority to enter into ye said Church of Kidderminster, one some convenient day before ye 29th of March instant, and to take a view of ye place soe designed for ye erectinge of ye said Gallery as is above specified, and that you certify to us, or our lawfull Surrogate at our next Court being ye 29th instant under your hands whether ye erectinge of ye said Gallery, in ye said place will in any way prejudicall to y^{e} said Chancell, or hinder y^{e} light thereof, or seperate the same from y^{e} Church, or hinder y^{e} persons who sit in y^{e} said Chancell from hearinge y^{e} Minister's performance of Divine Service.

Given under our seale of office y^{e} 15th day of March 1682.

Tho Vernon Reg$^{r.}$

On the reverse side, the end of each line being decayed, appears to be the Commissioners report.

Wee whose names are subscribed herewith humbly certify all whom it may concern . . . . pursuant to the trust and authority within to us given wee have this day viewed the place . . . . parish Church of Kidderminster, intended for the erection of a Gallery within . . . and doe conceive that the erecting of the said Gallery, according as it is proposed . . . . the said Church, from the Chancell and will in any way hinder the light . . . . and whether it will hinder the hearing of those that shall sit in the said . . . . same shall be erected wee are not able at present to judge. Witness our . . . . 22nd day of March Anno dni 1682.

Richard
Richard White (Vicar)
William Lewis
Edward Walker
Henry Toye

On the Margin of No. 7747 are the names of persons, evidently appointed to view site of said Gallery, viz.: Master Skinner, Master Tristram, Wr. White, Clerk, Edward Walker, Henry Toye, and William Lewis. Nos. 7747-8 have reference to same Gallery, and that Mr. Dobbins, as lay Rector is within his rights as to the hurt of those sitting in the Chancel. The missing part leaves it doubtfull as to the gallery, being in connection of Roodloft, prejudicial to the beholder, as well the hearer of the sermon in the distant pulpit, attached to one of the pillars on the North side of the Nave.

Hence, these documents show, that although Baxter's statement is ambiguous, it is true in fact, as being five parallel sittings in the South Eastern arcade of the said Church as concluded.

It is within the remembrance of many now living (1921) that a single tier of raised sittings did exist, faithfully depicted by a drawing upon the Chantry Wall of the said Church.

ESSAY TWO

THOMAS CAVE - HIS ESSAY ON BAXTER, BASED UPON MATHEW SYLVESTER'S BIOGRAPHY OF BAXTER, " CHIEFLY IN HIS OWN WORDS."

Note.—With reference to Page 61.

THERE were 3 several Ordinances of Parliament. "For the utter demolishing, removing, and taking away all Monuments of Superstition or Idolatry." Baxter's narrative being without date may imply either of the following: That of 1641, was but a prelude to those of August 28, 1643, and May 8, 1644, which ordained—"That the person or persons, making default, be fined 40s. for the use of the poor of the Parish." That of 1644, had in addition—"And that all organs, and the frames of cases wherein they stand in all Churches and Chappells aforesaid shall be taken away and utterly defaced, and none other hereafter set up in their places"; "and Fonts aforesaid be likewise utterly defaced, whereunto all persons within this Kingdome, whom it may concern, are hereby required at their peril, to yield due obedience." (*Scobell's Collections*). Knowing Baxter to be a Puritan Zealot by his non-mention, and silence, it can be inferred, *That no organ, was either before or during his ministry, in use in the Parish Church of Kidderminster.*

THOMAS CAVE.

RICHARD BAXTER

(1615–1662).

Part II.

FROM the reading of the preceding Part I, telling of Galleries erected in Kidderminster Parish Church, denoting a successful Ministry, while in the Town (1640-61) and Baxter's long association, in, and about that area, as well his early career, and historical events may be acceptable, and renew afresh, the story of a great struggle in defence of Civil and Religious Liberty in England's history at a critical period. The account herewith given, are chiefly Baxter's own words, given in his Life by his friend, M^r. Mathew Sylvester (Edition 1696), with such comments thought applicable of him as a youth, and a Man, susceptible to the frailties of the human race. His character as a religious Teacher, and his great influence in attempting a unity, which has hitherto been impossible in thought is left to other pens.

Baxter was born 15 November, 1615, at Rowton, co. Salop, he was named after his father, and grandfather. His father had a small freehold estate, but which by their gambling, was so encumbered with debt, as to leave but sufficient for their cares. Hence, his parents had but little to give in School learning, and that of the University, on which in his early ministry he had set his heart. Like other boys, the fruit stolen from other's orchards, was

Baxter p. 2.

sweet, foolish words, his actions bold, and irreverently, puffed up, and a love for money.

While a youth, he saw the evils of the life surrounding him, and he at once, except when the love of sport enticed him, given his aspirations to something higher, and better, and it would appear that his schoolmaster, Mr. John Owen, at the Free School at Uttoxeter had much influence in that direction. His school-mates, many of them, were above him in degree, as Sir Richard Newport's sons', but not in learning, and by their position obtained the scholarships to the University, which he took ill, and talked of leaving, but his Master tenderly, rebuked his pride, and gave him a lesson, "The shoemaker must not go beyond his last."

A saying, attributed to Apelles, a Grecian painter (B.C. 332) who placing a picture, which he had finished in a public place, stood by to hear the criticisms of the beholders. One day a cobbler observed a defect in the shoe which the painter corrected. The cobbler came next day, and encouraged by the success of his first remark, began to censure the leg of the figure, upon which the painter made the above remark, hence its origin.

Knowing the difference between good and evil, he began to consider whether his life was that taught by Scripture, and a conviction that he was sinful, he claims that by reading an old torn book, written by a Jesuit (Parsons), led him to the determination to be a Minister.

Failing entrance to the University from his school, his schoolmaster, having knowledge that the Chaplain (Mr. Richard Wickstead) to the Court at Ludlow, had an allowance granted to him, for the tuition of a scholar for the University, he with his parents' consent accepted the offer. It proved of no advantage to him, beyond having access to a good library, his Tutor being lax in giving him instruction, but he speaks of him kindly, and loved by him. The Court of the Lord President at Ludlow, was then in high repute, crowded with Law Officers, and their attendants, in suits of law before the Judges, and so he would be in continual contact with persons of worth and

Baxter p. 4.

intelligence. He was then but a youth about 17 years of age (1632) and can hardly be said to have attained to any fixed convictions, and while there he says that the Gentlemen of the Court had little else to do, but to gamble, and play dice, in which he set out to try his luck. In one game, in which he must have been infatuated, and more resolutely determined by the laughs of the byestanders, and his opponent, challenging 100 to 1 at one point of the game, and in response laid down 10s. to my 6d. spurred him on to become the winner. He suddenly imagined the Devil was enticing him on to become a Gambler, he returned the stake, and resolved never more to gamble while he lived. After a stay of about a year and half, he returned home, and filled for a few months the post of Master at his old School, at Uttoxeter, and having instruction in theology and general subjects, by a neighbouring clergyman. Recovery after a serious illness, and at times acting as a preacher, though but young—to the villages around, his friend Mr. Wickstead wrote advising him to forego all thought of the Church, and professed his influence to place him with Sir Henry Herbert, (of Ribbesford), Master of the Revels at the Court at Whitehall, and try his fortune thereat. Being of an ambitious mind, and with his parents' consent, he became an aspirant for Royal favour, and went to London. He was there but a short time, his serious mind disliking a stage play instead of a sermon, on the Lord's day, and his mother being ill, a fortunate excuse for his return home. It was while a youth, and at the places named, the reviling, and harshness to the Puritan, led him to enquire the cause of their position in the Church, he himself as yet having no scruples, as to the Articles of Subscription to the Church of England, nor against ordination. He particularly noted their piety, and their attempt to stem the moral corruption, then prevailing, and was drawn to them by being in accordance with his own conscience, and from thence he began to

Baxter p. 12.

Baxter p. 11.

examine the said Articles.

Baxter appears throughout his whole life to have been a weakly person, and subject to frequent illness, hence he was of a sad disposition, his every thought, word, or deed sinful, troubled for inward defects, and omissions, the want of vital duties, or grace in the soul.

Baxter p. 128.

Writers of the period record that very many of the Parish Ministers were illiterate, immoral, frequenters of ale houses, and neglectful in their ministerial duties to those under their charge.

I know not for what cause Baxter, on p 12, should tell, he himself as yet having had no connection with Kidderminster, viz. : " At Kiddermnster, the town being in want of fire, went all to shovel the way over the heath to Stourbridge, from whence their coals came, and so great, and sudden a storm of snow fell, as overwhelmed them, so that some perished in it, and others escaped their lives by getting into a little cote that standeth on the heath, and others escaped home with much ado." On p 11, he tells, " The snow was about the country at Christmas Day, and lasted till Easter." He gives the date of this occurrence as in 1634. The Kidderminster Parish Register records, " 1634, January 31st buryed Richard Reynolds whoe was starved in the snowe." " The same day was buryed John Bowyer starved in the snowe." " ffebruary, the first, buryed Thomas Wells starved in the snowe." The above dates correspond to 1635, new style.

It must have been as an itinerant preacher, that Baxter was brought under the notice of Mr. Richard Foley, senr. of Stourbridge, co Worcester. Mr. Foley by his marriage with Alice, daughter of William Brindley, of the Hyde Iron Works, near Stourbridge, was the progenitor of the family, most successful, and founder of the Foley fortunes. He died in 1657, aged about 80 years of age. Having recovered some lands called, " Our Lady's Lands "

Baxter p. 13.

lying in Dudley co Worcr. which had been granted in the time of Queen Elizabeth, to the then Vicar of Dudley, and 24 others in trust to the use, as well a school for ever, to be kept, found, and maintained in the said Borough of Dudley, as well other premises, and lands bequethed by others in 1629 etc., found much had been diverted to other uses, or the rents unpaid for many years. By a commission 21st November 1637, they were recovered, and Mr. Foley giving something of his own, he was allowed to choose the School Master, and Usher of Dudley Grammar School. A new School having been built, Baxter says, " By the means of James Berry, who lived in the house with me, and who had lived with Mr. Foley, he desired me to accept it, I thought it not an inconvenient condition for my entrance into life, because I might preach up and down in places that were most ignorant before presuming to take up a Pastoral charge. So to Dudley I went, and at the time of ordination Mr. Foley, and James Berry went with me to Worcester, where I was ordained by the Bishop (Thornborough) and had a licence to teach school, for which being examined I subscribed. Being settled with an Usher in the new school at Dudley, and living in the house of Mr. Robert Foley, Junr., I there preached my first public sermon in the Upper Church (St. Thomas)". He remained at Dudley about 9 months, he being yet a young man, restless, unstable, and liable to change, that of conformity most disturbing to his mind, and no doubt, but to his puritanic life, the reading each Sunday, the Order, issued in the late reign called the Book of Sports, of the people's indulgence, in all manner of pastimes, disorderly, and drunken after evening service, and which many of the most devout clergy refused to read, and who were suspended or deprived of their ministerial office in consequence. This reading is said to have been the test of puritanism, and a politic move on behalf of the high Church prelates.

Baxter p. 13.

1638.

Hence with matters of rite, and strict observance of the sabbath, and the threatening disruption between absolutism of the King, and liberty of Parliament, he cast about for a more congenial sphere for his labours. He tells he was invited to be assistant to Mr. Madestard, a grave, and serious ancient divine, very honest conscionable, and an excellent preacher, and in full accordance with his own disturbed mind, and having a wider field for his exertion. Bridgnorth being a peculiar of 6 parishes outside ecclesiastical jurisdiction, other than the triennial visitation of the Archbishop of Canterbury, it was fortunate for both, that the visitor, the persecuting Archbishop Laud, did not make visitation, for neither Baxter, or the Minister observed the rites of the Conforming Church. Baxter tells, " That the first thing that threatened him at Bridgnorth was the *et cetera oath*, and complaint was made by the parishioners of non-compliance with that Order."

Baxter p. 16

The *et cetera oath* was a series of canons made in convocation (1640) which filled up the measure of public wroth against the tyranny, folly, and rashness of Charles's Bishops which were greater than his own. These enjoined, or at least recommended some of the modern innovations, which had not got the sanction of authority (bowing, making the sign of the cross, the divine presence in the Eucharist, and other Romish practices) binding them to attempt no alteration in the government of the Church, by bishops, deans, archdeacons, etc. This oath was by the same authority enjoined to such of the laity that held ecclesiastical office. The King, however, on the petition of the Council of peers, at York, directed it not to be taken. The house of commons rescinded these canons with some degree of excess, on the other side, not only denying the right of convocation to bind the clergy, which had been exercised in all periods, but actually impeaching the bishops for a high misdemeanour on that account. (Hallams' Constitutional History of England. Vol. 2, p. 156-7.)

" A second danger, was when the Lord President of the Marshes, the Earl of Bridgwater, in his passage thro the Town, from Ludlow to the King in the North, on the Saturday. The most malicious persons in the town, went to him, and told him Mr. Madestard, and I, did not sign with the cross, nor wear a surplice, nor pray against the Scots, for which we had no command from the King, but

Baxter p. 17.

a printed form of Prayer from the Bishop. He told them he would come to the Church himself on the morrow, and see whether we would do these things, or not. Mr. Madestard, went away, and left the reader Mr. Swain, and myself in (charge or) danger. He had spoken for his dinner, and was ready to go to Church, but suddenly changed his purpose, and went away on the Lord's day, as far as Lichfield, requiring the accusers, and the Bailiff to send after him to inform him on what we did. On the Lord's day after evening service, they sent word to him at Lichfield that we did not conform, and though they boasted no less, than the hanging of us they received for answer, that he had not ecclesiastical jurisdicton, and could not meddle with us, and the Bailiffs, and accusers, had no more wit, than to read the letter to me, that I might know how they were baffled." "Thus I continued my liberty of preaching the Gospel at Bridgnorth, about a year, and a three-quarter, considering my liberty to be a great mercy to me, in those troublesome times. The rebuff administered by the Lord President, to the accusers of Baxter, and Mr. Madestard, by his telling them plainly, he should take such order in the business as he thought fit, emboldened Baxter in his course, meanwhile keeping in knowledge of the disputes, and divisions in State and Church, but allying himself to no particular party as yet, and I am of opinion that had the abuses, in the Church been remedied he would have been on the Royalist side during the incoming struggle. The Parliament that met in November 1640, early resolved on measures against ecclesiastical, as well temporal grievances, and appointed a Committee to receive complaints against scandalous Ministers, such as were ignorant drunken, and otherwise unfit. And Kidderminster was one of the towns, sending up a petition against their Minister." The vicar, Mr. George Dance, they articled against as one that was utterly insufficient for the Ministry,

Baxter p. 18.

presented by a Papist, unlearned, preached but once a quarter, which was so weakly, as exposed him to laughter, and persuaded them that he understood not the very substantial articles of Christianity, that he frequented ale houses, and had sometimes been drunk, that he had turned the Table Altarwise, with much more such as this.

Baxter p. 20.

The vicar had a curate under him in the Town whom they also accused. And a Curate at a Chapel in the Parish (Mitton) a common tippler, and a drunkard, a railing quarreller, and an ignorant insufficient man, who understood not the common points of the children's catechism .... and his trade in the week-days was unlawful marriages. The people put this petition into the hands of Sir Henry Herbert, Burgess for Bewdley. The vicar knowing his insufficiency, and hearing how two similiar cases had sped, he desired to compound the business with them, and by the mediation of Sir Henry Herbert, and others it was brought to this. That he should allow instead of his present curate in the Town, £60 per annum, to a Preacher whom 14 of them nominated, should choose, and that he should not hinder the Preacher from preaching whenever he liked, and that he himself should read Common Prayer, and do all else that was to be done. And so they preferred not their petition against him, nor against his curates, but he kept his place which was worth to him £200 per annum, allowing that £60 out of it to their lecturer. To perform this he gave a bond of £500." .....The 14 after hearing one Mr. Lapthorn, invited Baxter from Bridgnorth.... " The Bailiff of the Town, and all the feoffees desired me to preach to them in order to a full determination. It was a full congregation, and a most convenient temple, an ignorant, rude, and revelling people for the greater part, who had need of preaching, and yet had among them, a small company of Converts, who were humble, godly, and of good conversation, and not much hated by the rest, and therefore the fitter to assist their teacher. As soon as I came to Kidderminster, and had preached there but one day, I was chosen *nemine contradicente*, for though 14 only had the choosing, they desired to please the rest."

He accordingly entered upon his office (that of many years' labour). Being then but 25 years of age. By what means did he so enrapture his audience? In his after years, he says "many popular sermons preached 20 years ago, were very rude, and undigested." "When I was young I was more vigorous, affectionate, fervent in preaching, Conference, and Prayer, my stile was more extempore, and lax, a very familiar moving voice, and utterance, my preaching did more affect the auditory than many of the last years, before I gave over preaching, but yet what I delivered was much more raw, and had more passages that would not bear the tryal of accurate judgments, and my discourses had both less substance, and less judgment than of late." A most candid confession and revealing him in the character of many revivalists who with a flowing tongue and fierce denunciations, sway the multitude, prone to rash assertions, and a mark for better informed persons than himself, ofttimes much opinionated, dogmatic, and intolerant to other religious views than his own.

Baxter p. 124.

Being of a gloomy disposition, and his severe strictures against amusement of any kind, made many bitter against him. He was he tells "fraught with terror, and vain talk, imagining the Devil hindered his work, and stirred up wicked men against him."

On the occasion of (Holy Thursday) fair at Kidderminster, he says, "The Town was formerly given up to vanity, in which they brought forth the painted figures of giants, and such like foolery, to walk about the streets with (probably his Guy), and though I said nothing against them, the rabble of a more vicious sort, had still some spleen against me as part of their game, and the ignorant sort were raging mad against me for preaching the doctrine of original sin, and telling that infants before regeneration, had so much guilt, and corruption as made them loathsome in the eyes of God, whereupon they vented it abroad in the country. That I preached God hated, or loathed infants, so that they railed at me as I passed thro' the streets. The next Lord's day, I cleared, and confirmed it, and showed them that if this was not true, their infants had no need of Christ, of baptism, or renewal of the Holy Ghost, and I asked them whether they durst say, that their children were saved without a Saviour, and were no christians and why they baptized them, with much more to that purpose, and afterwards they were ashamed, and as mute as fishes." On p. 91 of his life, he tells more plainly his action, as to infant baptism, which is, that at a presentation of an infant for baptism, that unless the parents, whom he deemed sinners, refused to confess their sin, and were penitent, he refused baptism to the child, and the visitation of their sins upon the infant's head. A doctrine which to present thought, most repugnant. From a study of Parish Registers it corroborates what I have formerly attributed to negligence by the Minister, a definite denial of such child's existence being entered as of right in the Parish Register, a most unworthy action, and a perverse interpretation of Christ's saying, " Suffer little children to come unto me, etc." No wonder the ignorant sort, as he repeatedly calls others of different views to his own, in the parish, should speak ill of him,. and some few when found out, were bound over for their future good conduct.

Baxter p. 24.

It was in 1640–1, that apart from his ministry, he was compelled to consider in the manner, in which he should take part, then agitating the kingdom, but while upholding monarchy, his feelings were decidedly in favour of the Parliament, and he was looked upon with suspicion, and the mob assailed him in the street, with cries of, " Down with the Roundheads." Knowing his repugnance to Popery, and the Laudian innovations into the Church, fear perchance caused him to fight shy of any action, beyond reading out in the Parish Church, the Order sent down by Parliament, 1641, for the demolishing of all Statues and Images of the three persons in the Blessed Trinity, and of the Virgin Mary, Crosses and pictures which should be found in Churches, and the Crosses in Churchyards." He obeyed this order, thinking it came from just authority, but meddled not in it, leaving it to the Churchwarden to do what he thought good. The Churchwarden (an honest, sober, quiet man) seeing a Crucifix upon the Cross in the Churchyard, set up a ladder to reach it, which being too short, and while away to get a longer, a crew of drunken riotous party of the Town (poor journeymen, and servants) took the alarm, and ran altogether with weapons to defend the Crucifix, and the Church images of which there were divers left since the time of Popery. The report spread among them, I was the chief actor, and it was me they sought, but I was walking about a mile out of the Town, or else I suppose, I should have ended my days. When they missed me, and the Churchwardens both, they went raving about the streets to seek us. Two neighbours, hearing they sought my life, ran in among to see if I was there, were both knocked down, and I think never perfectly recovered the hurt. When they had roamed about half-an-hour, and met with none of us, and were safely housed, I came in from my walk, and hearing the people cursing at me in their doors, I wondered what was the matter, but quickly found out how fairly I had escaped." Hence this ignorant, and drunken crew, saved from destruction, that solitary shaft, still standing like a sentinel near the Chancel Door on South side of the Church, as well as what appears

Baxter p. 40.

by Mandates, Nos. 7747—7748 given in the preceding Part 1, to have been the Rood Gallery, at the division of the Chancel, and nave in the Parish Church, which objects to Puritans were likewise superstituous. The next Lord's day he says, "I dealt plainly with them, and told them, seeing they requited me as to seek my blood, I was willing to leave them, and save them from that guilt. But the poor souls were so amazed, and ashamed, that they took on sorrily, and were loth to part with me." Previous to the afore Order, "Parliament had made an Order for all persons to take a protestation to defend the King's person, Honour, Authority, Power, and Privileges of Parliament, Liberties of the Subject, and the Protestant Religion I obeyed in joining with the Magistrate in offering to the people, the Protestation." "About this time, the King's Declaration of array, was read in our market place, and the reader (a violent Country Gentleman) seeing me pass the street, stopped, and said, "There goes a Traitor" without giving a reason for it." "And when the Commission of array was set afoot, the rage of the Rioters, was greater than before. If a stranger passed in many places that had short hair, and a civil habit, the Rabble cried down with the Roundheads, and some they knocked down in the open street." The Town is thus shown, divided into two factions, and he says, "the Vicar's brook (which is that arm of the River Stour, flowing by the present G. Post Office), was the division of the good, and evil in the parish." That is to say, the foreign led by Sir Ralph Clare, C.B., High Steward of the Borough, as well Lord of Caldwell, were for the King, and the Puritan party in the Boro, for the Parliament, and which appears in conformity with after results.

Baxter p. 40.

Baxter p. 85.

Independently of military service by Knight tenure, an Act 5, Philip and Mary, it was obligatory, on each person accordingly to their estate, as to the provision of their keeping arms for defence of the kingdom. It was abrogated, James I., and in 1638 a fresh order made for the like purpose. To the Lord Lieutenants of the Counties, whose office gave him command of the militia as vice regent of his sovereign, responsible for public order. This power of mustering and training to arms at this period 1638 was manifestly vested in the King.

It is well known that prior enactments were in force, such as produced our Archers of Cressy, and Agincourt, and which at the period of which we write were termed train-bands, our modern militia. At a Court view of Frankpledge, and Court Baron, of the neighbouring Manor of Wolverley held 24th of October 1632. The inhabitants thereof were presented by reason of their not practicing with bows and arrows, and throwing darts to catch crows, and other flying birds, according to statute. They are fined 6$^{s.}$ 8$^{d.}$ Kidderminster would be under same enactment, and their practice land, probably that now known as the Park Butts. That the Inhabitants were trained in arms is evident from a Byelaw of the Borough, dated 14 Dec$^{r.}$ 1640. Clause 9. " It is ordered, that all Burgesses, and Inhabitants of the said Borough shall from time to time, upon request, aid and assist the said Bailiff, the Justice of the Peace, and the Constables of the said Borough, for the time being, in the execution of their offices at the time of any assault, affray, misdemeanour, or other just occasion upon pain of 10$^{s.}$ for each default. And to that end they the said Burgesses and Inhabitants, and every of them shall have, and keep in his, or her shop, or shops, or houses, convenient, ready, and prepared, a staff, club, bit or halbert, upon pain of 10$^{s.}$ for every month, they shall be defective, after this publication." Was this one means of preparing for the coming affray ? In the Parish Chest is an " Accompt of money disbursed by William Hodgkis, constable of Kidderminster foreign, concerninge the trayned soldiers, dated 1685."

Imp$^{s.}$ for mending M$^{r.}$ Bowyer's armes 6$^{s.}$ 0$^{d.}$—for collers (colours) 19$^{s.}$ 0$^{d.}$—for 2 belts 6$^{s.}$ 0$^{d.}$—spent in y^{e} field wth y^{e} souldiers 1$^{s.}$ 0$^{d.}$ at the deliveringe y^{e} collers (colours) 1$^{s.}$ 0$^{d.}$—for scouringe pikes, and musquetts 2$^{s.}$ 6$^{d.}$—p$^{d.}$ for 2 supplies for press money 2$^{s.}$ 0$^{d.}$—for the warr$^{t.}$ 1$^{s.}$ 0$^{d.}$—itm. charges for 6 supplies 8$^{s.}$ 0$^{d.}$—spent chardgings in supplies 2$^{s.}$ 6$^{d.}$—p$^{d.}$ at 2 meetings about y^{e} souldiers 6$^{s.}$ 0$^{d.}$—p$^{d.}$ 9 trayne souldiers for 7 days at 1$^{s.}$ 6$^{d.}$ per day, £4 14 6—for a month's pay advance at 2$^{s.}$ 0$^{d.}$ per day £25 4 0—for powder and bulletts 13$^{s.}$ 4$^{d.}$ for an order to distrayne for my levy and my chardges 8$^{s.}$ 0$^{d.}$—for my chardges 5 days at Worc$^{r.}$ 16$^{s.}$ 0$^{d.}$—for wrighting the book, and accompts 6$^{s.}$ 0$^{d.}$—Total £34 17 6.

It is evident from the preceding pages that Baxter was not the man to promote peace among his people, and in after years, confesses to his ignorance in politics without which the true nature of Government, Laws, and Judgment in general, and the Laws of Nature, show how unfit one is to write about Christian Law, Government, and Judgment, and so ignorant in Divine teaching, such was his conception of a M$^{r.}$ George Lawson's criticism of his Saints' Rest. A Book written after his resignation of Army Chaplain, and

Baxter p. 108.

while recruiting his health, before again entering upon his Ministry in the Town at the end of the War,

Hence this unrest in the Town, his friends readily perceived was by Baxter's action therein, and they advised him to go away from the Town, he going to Gloucester, that city and county being almost wholly, being for the Parliament, while Worcestershire, with few exceptions being for the King, wherever he went, and at all times, he is shown as desirous of controversy. It appears that while there, he for the first time beheld an Anabaptist, in the flesh, a sect at that time taking root, and flourishing in the Parliaments of the Interregnum, and in the Army. This absence from Kidderminster was interpreted as a proof of guilt, or that he was against the King, and after an absence of a month, his friends of Kidderminster went to bring him home, it not being wise to stay away, and bidding his new made friends farewell, so returned to Kidderminster.

Baxter p. 42.

He found the Town still disturbed, and it was evident the Bailiff, and Chief Burgesses of the Town, could, or would not restrain those drunken sots, who were like unloosed mastiffs, and flew at all in their way. Baxter consoled himself by the knowledge of such joining the King's army, were quickly killed, so that scarce any returned from the War. The Leaders of the Rival factions in the Town, are taken to be Sir Ralph Clare for the King, and Mr. Daniell Dobbins for the Parliament. History tells the preparations made by each party for the struggle, the terms of peace made to the King, termed by him, as ignominious, and only to be decided by the sword. Charles with a number of adherents raised his standard at Nottingham, August, 22—1642, and which he kept flying until September 13th, during which period, he was advised to come to terms, with the House, to which he refused assent with the approval of his Counsellors.

It may readily been seen, what class favoured each

party. Those holding by feudal tenure (Knight service) being called upon by the Crown, and many of the leading gentry with their retainers, not necessarily the drunken sots, said by Baxter, which his puritanic mind belittles. That of Parliament, embraced a few of said tenants, small freeholders, sturdy yeomen, and traders in the large cities and towns.

The Parliamentarian forces, well equipped under command of the Earl of Essex, marching from London northward, arrived in due course at Gloucester, and several of his regiments are said to have been quartered in, and about Kidderminster. In the meanwhile the Royal forces crossed the Kingdom to Wales, which with the bordering counties of Salop, Hereford and Worcester, were favorable to his cause, and on arriving at Shrewsbury, intending to continue his journey to Oxford, each party augmenting their forces as they went along. The disorder in the Town increasing, and his partizanship well known, he instead of remaining to be a martyr, like to the unworthy shepherd, left his flock to the mercy of those whom he deemed illiterate, and unfit, and from now absent for some years, retiring to Inkborough, where the advance guard of the Earl of Essex's army had arrived on its way from London, to block up Sir John Byron in Worcester city. This advance guard lay in a meadow at Powick, above a mile from the city, and his friends, and countrymen, being levied for provisions, he must need go out to see it, his curiosity being aroused, and no doubt hoping for its success. Whether it was from false information, or not, of the Royalists going away. Those of Essex's guards determined to go forward in pursuit, and having passed thro' a narrow lane, into an open field, found themselves before the King's horse, under command of Prince Rupert, whom they thought miles away, who at once charged them, killing many, and the rest fled in terror to Pershore, where part of

1642

epr. 23 1642.

Essex's force lay, they also taking alarm, thinking the Royalists were in pursuit, fled to the advancing body, to which Baxter also fled, his high hope dashed. And he says, "This sight quickly told me of the vanities of Armies, and how little confidence could be placed in them." Prince Rupert, having relieved Byron, went in direction of the Royal forces, and Essex, marching on to Worcester, the advance part of his force entered Kidderminster, and Baxter in protection of the regiments of Col. Essex, Lord Wharton, and Sir Henry Cholmeley, came in, but for a short time. He enumerates the number of Chaplains to the Army, and the civility he received, and appears to have had an high opinion of them as "famous, excellent divines."

Baxter p. 42.

It was during this short stay in the Town, that news was brought that the Royal scouts had been seen on the Top of Kinver Edge, near Kidderminster, its army marching from Wolverhampton, on the way to Oxford. It was expedient for Essex's advance to retire on to the main body at Worcester, and in their haste leaving several carriages with arms, behind them, and which on the arrival of the King's forces in the vicinity, some entered, and taken them away, on information by some of the inhabitants.

The Royal army continuing on its course by way to Banbury, found itself confronted by Essex's forces at Edge Hill, near Kineton, co. Warwick. One writer says, it was a cold, grey, silent Sunday morning, 23rd October, 1642, the Church bells ringing out the summons for worship from many an hoary Church Tower, in the plains below. And in the afternoon of the same day, facing each, the silence was broken, and the conflict began, night was closing in, both sides exhausted and the death struggle ceased. Baxter tells, that this was on the Sunday, after his leaving Kidderminster, and was preaching at Alcester, co. Warwick, and as he was so engaged, the people heard the Cannon, and that the Armies were engaged, when sermon was done (in the afternoon), the report was more audible, which made us all long to hear of the success. About sun setting, many troops fled through the Town, telling that all was lost on the Parliament side, the carriages taken, and wagons plundered before they came away, and none that followed brought any other news. The fact being that Prince Rupert had routed and pursued one wing of Essex's army, and plundered the wagons, and the opposite wing of Parliament had driven off that of the Royalists, killed Sir Edmund Verney, and taken from him the Royal Standard, afterwards regained by Captain John Smith. The killed and those taken prisoners by each side being numerous, and the victory may be said to be undecided, though, said by Baxter to be for the Parliament. All night the two armies in the cold keen winds lay under arms, and on the trampled meadows lay nearly 2,000 (some say 1,200) men, stretched lifeless, and the next morning stood facing each other, each averse to continue the fight. Baxter says, the next morning about 4 o'clock, news being brought to them of the result of the battle, he, and others wishing to see the field of Battle, journeyed to Edgehill, and behold in its position, Parliament's men, and on the hill side opposite that of the King. Essex retired with his Army, to attend to his wounded, to Warwick Castle, the King continuing his course to Banbury.

Baxter p. 43.

May's History of Parliament, p. 176, and military Parliamentary Leaders, Ludlow, and Lord Wharton who were in the battle, say the military consequences were to the King, and by Essex's injudicious conduct after the battle, strengthened the King's side many neutral joining him.

Baxter's position was now beset with trials, not daring to live at home, at the mercy of every individual, and having neither money or friends, nor anyone to find him a safe refuge, and having no means to satisfy for diet, and entertainment, and the City of Coventry, being wholly for Parliament, he went there, with an idea the war would soon be over, and he to return again home. It being a walled city, and strongly garrisoned by men from Birmingham, Nuneaton, Hinckley, and others in the Midland area, many of whom had gone there for safety, in combination, and while there many from Kidderminster entered, and were compelled to take up arms for its defence to get their bread, as well about 30 Ministers who had fled there for safety from soldiers, and popular fury. While there the Committee, and Governor offered him the Chaplaincy of the garrison, and to live in his house preaching once a week, and on the Lord's day to the soldiers, which offer suited his needs. Essex had previously given this office to a Mr. Aspinwall, who had by some way displeased the Committee, and Governor, who had discharged him, which caused unpleasure on his taking the place. After a residence of over a year, the area in Shropshire in which his father dwelt was being plundered by each party in turn of occupation, and not having seen him for some time, went with a few friends to see, and relieve him, having obtained leave of absence for a few weeks, and then to return. As in Gloucester, so he found in Coventry, others of a different religious thought to himself, whom he terms, Sectaries, of whom the Anabaptists appear to him most guilty of error and schism. Being a dominant, and aggressive controversialist, he appeared always to be forward in maintainance of his own view.

Baxter p. 44.

Baxter p. 45.

The war dragging on slowly to Parliament's view, and it was observed, as well as known, that the Parliamentary Commanders, Essex and Manchester, were for monarchy, and that in time, it would be restored, peace made, and their demands admitted. Their removal fomented by Cromwell in the Army, and Sir Harry Vane in the House, and that the army should be remodelled was resolved upon, the real purpose being withheld from the former commanders. After a great debate, a Committee was chosen to frame what was called the "Self-denying Ordinance" by which the Members of both houses were excluded from all civil, and military employment, except a few who were named. It was passed in the House of Commons, the Peers seeing it was levelled against them, and though rejected once by them, dared not again reject it. The Ordinance passed both Houses, April 3, 1645. Essex, Warwick, Manchester, Denbigh, Waller, and many others, resigned their commands receiving the thanks of Parliament for their good services, and a Pension of £10,000 a year settled upon Essex.

And from now the restoration of the King upon any terms, was very slender.

At the commencement of the war, it may be said within a certain degree of truth, there was but one non-conforming body, called Presbyterians, who denying scriptural authority of the Episcopal Order, whose government, and superintendence of its Ministers was not in an individual, but in a synod or presbytery of this class was Baxter, and in Parliament, and a great part of the nation were a considerable majority.

From this body, arose a body of faithful men, who regarded not the union of Churches, but that each congregation was independent in itself. They early begin to assert themselves in the reign of K. Charles I. as Independents. Of this class, were Cromwell, Hampden, and others, and at the time of this Self-denying Ordinance most assertive, and all seasons the most tolerant of the Christian Sects.

They were opposed to monarchy, maintained the equality of men, and order, in a republic quite free, and independent, as formed by the Puritan in new England. "The Presbyterian saw with dismay their growth, as favouring freer thought, while the Independents, with the numerous sectaries, nursed in the lap of presbyterianism, are said to number 176 heresies, and in this dis-union the Royalist's fondly believed, and rejoiced that one, or other of this party would seek assistance from them." "The Presbyterian zealots were systematically intolerant. A common cause made all sectaries tolerant." (Hallams' Const[l] Hist[y] Vol. 2, p. 269—271.)

And it was from this a different spirit arose which animated the Parliament's forces in the coming, and final contest. Parliament speedily raised an Army of 20,000 men, Sir Thomas Fairfax in command, and Baxter notes an alteration in his commission, which before ran (for defence of the King's person), which is now omitted to the army commission, being in that of the Parliament alone.

Baxter probably hints at the truth, in saying it was really in the hand of Oliver Cromwell. The fame of Cromwell had raised his regiment up to 14 troops, and which he now sub-divided to trusty commanders, his confidents were relatives, and close friends, one of whom was Major James Berry, Baxter's old friend at Dudley. By strict discipline, and non-appointments of Army Chaplains to many regiments (the former armies swarmed with them) many of the officers assumed the spiritual duty, with their military functions, and the private soldiers seized with a like spirit, entered into the fray with fanatical religious fervour, and in their camp, with vehement controversy.

The King having left Oxford to relieve certain Towns in the North, and having met with success, returned by way of Leicester, which Town, he assaulted and taken, on his march back to Oxford. Oxford, during the King's absence was invested by Fairfax, who abandoned the seige, and went forward to meet the King, and give him battle. The King having advanced to Daventry, by way of Harborough, suddenly retired on hearing of Fairfax's advance to more favorable position, and in hope of augmented forces, and each army suddenly found itself within 6 miles of each other, near Naseby, co. Northampton, with such dire result as may be said to have decided the ultimate issue of the War.

Baxter p. 50.

Baxter being at Coventry, and news of the victory known to the garrison, tells that on awakening each morning, the news of Parliament's army, was commonly the first word he heard, and having a few friends in Cromwell's army, whom he had not seen for 2 years, and desirous to see whether they were dead, or alive, he set out to Naseby, and from thence to Leicester, to which Town, Parliament's forces had advanced, and retaken. His first night with his friends speedily shown him the power, and influence of these sectaries in the army, and the Presbyterian party of no influence, and going about among the soldiers, and imaging his influence as a regimental Chaplain, would help to restore it to its former influence, was invited by Colonel Whalley, to be his chaplain. But being Chaplain at Coventry, he must need return, and obtain permission, promising a reply. Laying before the Assembly of Ministers in Coventry, his impression of his need for going away, to which they, and the Governor gave consent, he sending word to Whalley of acceptance. On his entrance to the army, Cromwell coldly bid him welcome, but never after spoke to him while there, and the report speedily spread about, that there was a Reformer come into the Army to set them right, and to save Church, and state, with other jeers.

Baxter p. 52.

With the army, at Naseby and Leicester, was John Bunyan, the Bedfordshire tinker, serving as a common soldier. As a Baptist guilty of the grossest sin of schism, in Baxter's views. We do not know that they met, but a room was formerly shown near St. Nicholas's Church in Leicester, in which he is said to have preached.

Baxter's vain idea of the Army being corrupt, was on a par with his own seditious acts, and when opportunity offered to dispute with one, or other of the sectaries, his

Baxter p. 53.

Discourses when in the Army, being on Points of Santification and Christian experience. Some disputed with him on Civil and Religious matters, and oft hooted and hissed him down. Travelling westward with Whalley, seeing much fighting, we find that in the summer (20th May) 1646, Whalley laid siege to Worcester, and that he could, as being in the area of Parliamentary influence, run over and see his one time friends, in Kidderminster

and in the interval of a parley entered into a disputation with Dr. Warmstry, one of the dignitaries of the Worcester Cathedral. Baxter's argument being "That there is no difference between a Church, and any other common place." The result being that each differed in terms of Holiness. (Townsend's Diary of the Seige of Worcester, ed. by J. Willis Bund, p. 122.)

When the siege was over, having with joy seen Kidderminster, and his friends, they expecting him to return, and settle in peace with them. Being bound by agreement with the Committee at Coventry, he applied for release, which was granted, and after a few months' rest at various friends' houses he returned to Kidderminster, remaining there until his ejection in 1661-2, and the war may be said to have ended by the taking of Harlech Castle, N. Wales, in April 1648.

It was while recruiting his health, that those at Kidderminster had renewed their articles against their Old Vicar, and Curate, and that upon trial of the cause.

Baxter p. 79.

"The Parliament Committee sequestrated the place, but put no one in it, but put the profits of the place into the hands of divers of the Inhabitants to pay a preacher, till it was disposed of. They sent for me, and desired me to take it, which I flatly refused, and told them I would only take the Lecture, according to former agreement. After some delay in meeting with some one to their mind, they chose one, Mr. Richard Serjeant, to officiate, reserving the vicarage for some one fitter." A further appeal he likewise refused, the Magistrates and Burgesses, met him in the Town Hall, and he told them on what conditions.

He says, "That he was offered many hundred pounds per annum elsewhere, he was willing to continue with them in" my old Lecturer's place, which I had before the war, expecting they would make the maintainance a hundred pounds per year, and a House, and if they would promise to submit to that doctrine of Christ, which as his Minister, I should deliver to them, proved by the Holy Scriptures, I would not leave them. And that this maintainance should not come out of their own purses, nor any more of it out of the Tythes, save the £60, which the Vicar had bound himself to pay me. I undertook to procure an augmentation for Mitton (a chapel in the parish) of £40 per annum, which I did, and so the £60, and the £40, was to be part, and the rest I was to have nothing to do with. This Covenant was drawn up between us in Articles, and subscribed, in which I disclaimed the Vicarage, and Pastoral charge of the parish, and only took the Lecture.

And thus the sequestration continued in the hands of the Townsmen, who gathered the Tythes, and paid me (not a Hundred as they promised) but £80 per annum, or £90 at most, and house rent for a few rooms, in the top of another man's house, in the High Street, which is all I had in Kidderminster. The rest they gave to Mr. Serjeant, and about £40 per annum to the old Vicar, and £6 per annum to the King, and Lord for rent, beside other charges. But when they had long continued in this way, they feared lest someone else against their will, would get a grant of sequestration from the Committee, and therefore they went privately, and got an Order, for them to settle me in the Title, and never showed me, but kept it by themselves secretly, only to secure the place from a surprize, and themselves from repaying what they had disbursed. And thus it lay till the King's coming out of Scotland, to Worcester, they brought the Order to me to keep safe, they fearing to be called to account.

The foregiven telling of profits to the Minister of the Church. I think it desirable to give as not being generally known. That by a customal of Kidderminster, made in Court (Lord's) held on the hill (the Church hill) on the Monday next after the feast of S. Michael the Archangel, in the 7th year of the reign of King Edward the III., from the Conquest (1333). At this period there appears to have three Lords entitled to hold in one united Court for the whole Manor, in three separate holdings. The House of Mayden Bradley, co. Wilts, having patronage of the Church, and as Rector being one.

This customal tells of the tolls on entering, buying, and selling and the dues due by fines, the markets and fairs. Clauses reading "It is forbidden that Retailers buy nothing on fair days before the ringing of the bell, etc., under a fine of 40d. half to the lord, half to the Church." "Butchers ought not to sell leprous meat unless they show those who buy it what sort it is, or else set the said meat in a certain place upon a table covered by a linen cloth, with salt laid over it, as a sign of being leprous, under a fine of 40d. half to the lord, half to the Church, as often as it occurs." "It is also forbidden, that no man, or woman in the borough, make a pile of brushwood, hay, or straw, near their houses in the borough for the danger of fire, under a fine of 40d. half to the lord, half to the Church." "It is forbidden to any man or woman having pigs roaming about the streets, under a fine of 40d." "It is provided that all men, and women whosoever that have tenements shall have a vessel full of water near their doorway in summer, when it is dry weather for danger of fire, under a fine of 40d. half to the lord, half to the Church." "No one shall have dogs of a wanton disposition, on account of destruction to gardens, when they are open, and in neat order, under a fine of 40d. half to the lord, half to the Church." "All Burgesses, Tenants, or Inhabitants, are to keep their wethers in separate pastures, and inclosures under a fine of 40d. half to the lord, half to the Church." Thus showing provision for maintainance of the Minister and Church, at a far earlier period than 1646-7 in the Manorial Court.

Baxter says, that the whole time he lived in Kidderminster, tho' Parliament made order, that no Minister sequestered, should have his 5th part unless he removed out of the parish where he had been Minister, he never desired the old Vicar to remove from the vicarage house, nor even entered its doors, as his right, living in peace, and quietness with us," speaking no scandal, or ill word of him, though as will be seen hereinafter in 1660, awaking as if from sleepy innocence to his own again, instigated by others.

Baxter p. 97.

Baxter in no part of his narration speaks well of Cromwell, in contradistinction to others, who proclaim him a hero, and the King's death to him was treason and disloyalty.

After a few years peace, the Kingdom was disturbed by the appearance of Charles II. in the North, he being cordially supported by the Scotch. Eluding Cromwell's forces, he swiftly passed South, into England, being joined by friends in his course. The army passed most by Kidderminster (a field's breadth of) and the rest through it. Colonel Grove sent two or three messages to him, as from the King, to come to him, and after when at Worcester, some others were sent. But he says, " I was at that time under so great an affliction of sore eyes, that I was scarce able to see the light, nor sit, nor stir out of doors, and being so doubtful of the issue that followed, I thought if I had been able, it would have been no service to the King, it being so little, on such a sudden, that I could add to his assistance." A reply of fear, akin to that given by Bishop Compton, to James II. as to the invitation to William, Prince of Orange, to land in England, in defence of Civil and Religious Liberty, 1688 (Macaulay History of England, vol. II., p. 474). The Battle of Worcester (September 3, 1651) and its result, needs no re-telling, beyond disaster to the Royal cause. " The flying army, some of them, passed through the Town, and some by it. I was newly gone to bed, when the noise of the flying horse, acquainted us of the result, and some of Cromwell's Troops, that guarded Bewdley Bridge, having tidings of it, came into our Market place before my door (in High Street, nearly opposite the then Market Cross) to surprize these that passed by. And when so many hundreds of the flying came together, and the 30 Troopers, cried, Stand, and fired at them, they either hasted away, or cried quarter, not knowing in the dark, what number it was that charged them. And so many were taken there, as so few men could hold them. And till midnight the bullets were flying towards my door and windows, and the sorrowing fugitives hasting for their lives did tell us of the calamitousness of

Baxter 68-69.

Baxter p. 69.

war." The King in his flight is said to have passed through the parish, by way of Wolverley and Kinver, to Boscobel.

From the evidence of entries in the Parish Register of soldiers, slain or dying in the struggle, fighting was in, and about the Town, and good reason to infer their rendevoux, as most commodious, the Parish Church, and its Tower advantageous as a lookout for approaching forces. The entries being, viz. :—

1642. Oct$^{r.}$ **14th** buried one Thomas Kinge, a parliament souldier that broke his neck fallinge down the rock, towards Cursfield, into the holloway that leads to Bewdley.

1644. June **15th** buried a pliament souldier.

1644. Aug$^{t.}$ 22 buried James Phewtrell a souldier.

164$^{4}_{5}$. March 11 buried John Windie, alias Walker, whoe was slaine at Caldwall.

1645. July 1st buried a strange woman wounded at y^{e} battle in Leicestershire.

1645. November 8th buried a souldier, belonging to Sir Thomas Aston, slaine at Trimpley (a Royalist).

1645. December 4th buried John Dygons, a souldier under Cap$^{n.}$ Dungham.

1645. December 14 buried Giles another of his souldiers both slaine in y^{e} town.

164$^{5}_{6}$. March 13 buried Captain Charles Dungham, and Richard Kerby, one of his souldiers.

1646. April 8th interred Christopher Batal, a pliament souldier.

1646. April 19th buryed John Jones, a pliament souldier slaine at the skirmish at Worcester.

Having told of Baxter's re-entrance into the Town, he set about his ministerial duty, and that his bitterest enemies, that rose up in tumult against him, by their hatred of Puritans, had gone into the King's armies, and were killed, few of them returning again, and so there were few to make any great opposition to Godliness, and the great change in public affairs by the success in the Wars, and he thanked God for that he even under a usurper, whom he opposed, for the liberty and advantage to preach his Gospel with success, denied him under a King, to whom he had sworn and performed true subjection, and obedience, and of numerous other advantages he relates most fully.

Baxter p. 86.

When order was restored, "he found war had left ravages in his parish." "Many fathers, and brothers had fallen in battle." "The Industry of the Town had become sluggish, and the religion of many had grown cold, and faint." Yet in after time, he tells that on the Lord's day, there was no disorder, and as one passed along the streets, they might hear an 100 families singing psalms, or repeating sermons, and always a full attendance at Church, which could well be accounted for by following Byelaw of the Borough made 14 December 1640.

Baxter p. 84.

The 12th Byelaw of that date enacts, "It is ordered, and agreed, that the Churchwardens, and Constables of the said Boro', or any of them by order of the said Bailiff, or Justice of the Peace, for the time being every Sonday, or holy day, or other solemn day as shall be expedient, at morning and evening prayer. Immediately after the beginning of the 2nd lesson, shall go out off the Church and make diligent search into all Taverns, Inns, Alehouses and Victuallers, in the said Boro', for any person, or persons as shall be in the same at the time of divine service, or sermon. And if there be householders, men of worth, the Churchwardens to take special notice, and cause them to be presented to the Ordinary. And if there be idle and vagrant persons, or of no worth or ability, then the Constable shall arrest them, and bring them before the Bailiff, or Justice of the Peace for the time being to receive punishment agreeable to justice. And if the Constable, and Churchwardens, make default by neglect, partiality, or other causes. That they, and every of them so offending be fined 5 shillings each.

The use of Book of Common Prayer was abolished in February 164$\frac{4}{5}$, and a Directory for Publick Worship of God, throughout the Three Kingdoms of England, Scotland and Ireland together with an Ordinance of Parliament, and for the establishing, and observing of this Perfect Directory throughout the Kingdom of England, and Dominion of Wales. And it would be this Service used by Baxter, in his Ministration at Kidderminster. It gave a large discretionary use to the Minister as to the order, of the Service, the reading of the Scriptures, and the different sacraments of Baptism, and the Lord's Supper, and also firmly established the Presbyterian, and the Independents in the parish Churches, and to their endowments. The rite of Baptism was not in the old form, and at the font, but by or from a basin of water poured, or sprinkled on the face of the child, the sign of the cross not acknowledged, as being superstitious, the solemnization of matrimony, and the Lord's Supper, in almost accordance of superseded Book. From the period of this Ordinance, and the terms of Baxter's appointment as Lecturer, Mr. George Dance would be the proper register of entries in the Parish Register but the Kingdom being in an unsettled condition that scarce a parish Register can be said to be complete by the suppression of Episcopal Church Government, and the possession of even a Book of Common Prayer, a crime. From these facts, correct registration may be said to have been impossible, and that it was not until the Ordinance of 1653, that any regularity was again attained. By this Act, the Ministers were ordered to give up the parish Register to a layman, to be chosen by the householders of the parish before the 22 September, 1653, to be called the Parish Register. The Registers of the Parish, appear (by my transcription) to be fairly well kept during the period of this discruption 1640-61, but prior to this Ordinance, no Minister records the correctness of each page, as required by Statute. By this Ordinance, a magistrate performed service of marriage.

The entry in Kidderminster Register reads: " A True, and pfect Register of all birthes of children, weddings and burials of all sorts w'hin the Towne, and pryshe of Kidder-minster, in the countie of worcester, ffrom, and after the 29h day of September, Anno Dmi 1653, by Edward Climar, late before chosen, and Elected Register by vote of the sd townsmen, and pryshenars, at a publique meetinge upon notice given for the same purpose, and afterwards the sd Register was sworne by me Lawrence Pearsall, then Justice of the peace, in the sd Borough attendinge, etc. an Act of pliament of the 24h of August in the sd yeare 1653." In this registration a more correct record can be obtained, by the date of birth being given, instead of day of baptism, which may be days, or weeks as afore done. Marriages from surrounding areas, were not only announced in Church, three several Sundays, but proclaimed in the several cities, and market Towns, on three several market days in the market, the spot in the Town being at the High Cross at foot of High Street near to the pavement at entrance to the Market Hall.

There are 327 such marriages recorded, beginning in 1653, and the last entry December 2d 9h 16h 1660. The first, and last entry having reference to same family, Doolittle, a Clothier of the Town. There does not appear to be any proof of any single entry being in Baxter's hand-writing.

He says "The congregation was usually so full, that five galleries had to be built soon after he came, the Church very capacious, and the most commodious, and convenient, that ever he was in." In Part I., the manner of these galleries is discussed, showing the position in the S.E. arcade of the nave, the site of the Chantry of St. Katharine the patroness of which, her tomb, built in the south wall, and the finials of the shrine, damaged for support of said Galleries. A floor slab in said S.E., covering grave of Baxter's opponent in the Town, old Sir Ralph Clare, C.B., who was buried April 1670. Of him he says, that he

[Baxter p. 94.] hindered by his position his mission, more than a multitude of others could have done, he was an old man of great courtship, and civility, very temperate as to diet, apparel, and sport, and would seldom swear any louder, than by his troth, and shown to him personal reverence, and respect, beyond his desert, and conversed together in love, and [Baxter p. 11.] familiarity, yet having no relish of this preciseness and extempore prayer, and so much ado about heaven, and liking his own course of religious life, coming to Church [p's. 157-162.] but once on the Lord's day, *abstaining from the sacrament except but in the old way*, and a great part of the parish followed his example. His civility, and yielding much beyond others of the Royalists, sending his family to be catechized, and instructed, did show example with the worst to do the like. A tribute of respect for a conscientious man, lately delivered from prison for loyalty to his King, by Baxter's one time friend James Berry, who was now as Major General of the West Midland Counties, and North Wales, to protect all interests of the state, both civil and religious, and prevent seditious acts and preaching, and to Baxter after that appointment (1655) a thorn and [Baxter p. 97.] restrictive agent. Baxter speaks of him sneeringly as a servant (Clerk in an Ironworks), his reign modest but short, hated and scorned by the gentry that had known his inferiority, and that he had better have had other area, as he was only honored through fear, an insinuation by a Minister, of a man, who justly, and without harshness, exercised his duty, as honestly and conscientious as the accuser. Baxter's spleen probably arose from the following circumstances. When Chaplain in the Army, he chose to think, he had right to sit in military deliberations, and was discountenanced by Cromwell, and the Chief Officers of his mind which kept him a stranger from their Councils, and his one time friend, one of the chiefs, never once visited [Baxter p. 57.] him, and he taunts him as forsaking his old opinions, and calls his old friend, an ignorant, misguided man. He acknowledges him as a man of good natural parts, especially mathematical, and mechanical, no mean qualities. Berry thinking probably with some truth, that the Old Puritan Ministers were dull, self conceited, men of a lower form, and the Sectaries much higher than formerly, so in like did he see fuller Civil, and Religious Liberty than Baxter. (After the Restoration, Berry lay for some years imprisoned in Scarborough Castle).

One of the advantages claimed as Minister was his Weekly Lecture, and monthly disputations, attended by the Ministers of a large area, promoting unity, as well reverence, and of great value. Another was the quality of the sinners of the place. "There were two drunkards almost next door to me, who, the one by night, the other by day, did every week, roar and rave in the street like madmen, and after being either in the stocks, or gaol, were as bad as ever as soon as they came out, and were of that sin most abhorred." Another was Church discipline, penitence and confession, and amendment of life, and the keeping away from the Town all sects and such as do err. He tells that one of the drunkards aforementioned being cast out from Church communion, did stand in the market place when drunk, crying out, rage and curse at his door, following him to Church, laying violent hands on him in the Churchyard, with purpose to kill him, seizing his cloak with his hands, which being loose, escaped into the Church from his fury (it being Fair day), and some strangers in the Churchyard, drag'd him to the magistrate, and the stocks, and who ever after had evil intentions against him. Another help to him, was that the people were not rich. The rich he terms, proud and obstinate, the poor rich in faith. The common trade of the Town was stuff-weaving, which found work for all. None of the Tradesmen were rich, their trade finding them little else beyond food,

axter
0-91.

and raiment. The magistrates were few, of them worth above £40 p. an., and many not half as much. Three or four of the richest, and thriving masters in the trade, got but £500 to £600 in 20 years, and may be lost £100 by a bad debt. The generality of the master workmen, but little better than their workmen only they laboured not so hard.

The following Byelaw explains much of which Baxter gives no relation.

A Byelaw (No. 14) was made 23rd of August 1650, as follows, viz.: Forasmuch as the Society of Weavers of the Stuffs, called Kidderminster Stuffs, have received of late much damage in their reputation of trading, by the covetousness, and irregularity of some others, of the same profession within the said Boro' who for their own advantage have done a private trade of the same stuffs, deceitfully made both for measure and workmanship. By which means a scandal is fixed upon the said Trade, the Traders therein much disparaged, the trade decayed, and the poor increased who formerly by their labour therein were supported and maintained. For the regulation hereof, and to the end the said trade and profession may require its credit (now so much impaired) the poor as formerly set to work, and relieved, and that each man may in love, and charity live neighbourly one with the other. It is therefore, thought fit, and ordained that from now, no master of, and in the said trade of Weavers, nor likewise any of the Trades, belonging to the several Companies (Weavers, Taylors and Shoemakers) aforesaid shall take any apprentice to any of their trades, but shall first request the Wardens of the said Fraternity Society, Company, or Fellowship therewith who shall take care to have him bound according to the laws of the realm, etc. Byelaw 15 is a restriction as to keeping by any master (unless for good causes) of more than 3 looms for Linseys, Woolseyes, for a term of 3 years, and that each loom shall, if it conveniently may, weave a piece a week, 6 quarters wide and 24 yards long for which piece the journeyman that works thereupon shall weekly have 5 shillings during the said time, and so proportionally for other breadths and lengths. Byelaw 16, that no Tradesman of the Company, or Fellowship of the Weavers, shall henceforth sell any of the said stuff, but shall be first viewed, and allowed by the Warden, or Wardens of the said Company, or by a man of judgment in the trade. "To search, view, size and seal the said Stuff according to breadth, length, goodness, and firm colours, at such times and places agreed upon, etc." Any violation of this byelaw, the half of the value of the Stuff or Stuffs so sold to be to the use of the said Company of Weavers.

As a man ofttimes, slandered and defamed, but with unstained character, with sympathetic endeavour to alleviate all ills, whether of the mind, or of the body, for he was no mean physician (though savouring superstition) for he says, that beyond the allotment of his weekly duties in the parish, which appear full, he was forced for 5 or 6 years by the people's necessity to practice Physick, being forced by a disease to advise them, to save their lives. And because he never took payment from anyone he was so crowded with patients, that at times 20 would be at his door. This of itself endeared him to his people, and encouraged him greatly, by their attendance at service, and kindly support in the work he had so much at heart. Like as John Wesley considered the world as his parish, so did Baxter, and by his assistant Ministers, Richard Serjeant, Joseph Read and Thomas Baldwin (Laus Deo Bawlden in Dean and Chapter of Worcester's Parliamentary Survey 1649-50, as Incumbent of Wolverley) do duty to a parish over 20 miles in circuit. An old document, some two centuries old (in the Parish Chest) tells that the then Parish was divided into 3 parts for taxation purposes, the whole in charge of one vicar, prior to the ecclesiastical sub-divisions now seen. The mention of punishment in the stocks of those annoying Baxter is an old punishment shown by Statutes 23 and 25 Edward III. (1349-52) to be used for any servant, or labourer found wandering in any city or town. They were usually near to the Churchyard. That there were more than one in Kidderminster parish is evident from the constable's accounts (1750) in the Parish Chest, viz.: " for mending the stocks at Mitton 4$^{d.}$ . . p$^{d.}$ M$^{r.}$ Thomas Beck for making a new pair of stocks at Ribbenhall, 14$^{s.}$ 0$^{d.}$

axter
. 83.

axter
. 89.

Among those attending his Lectures, was M$^{r.}$ John Tombs, of Bewdley, reputed the most learned, and able Anabaptist in England, and although correspondence passed between them, all debate about Infant Baptism was avoided, until at last a debate was forced. So, at a meeting in his Church, on January 1st, in a crowded Church, the disputation began, the subject being, " Infant right to Church Membership to their Right to [by] Baptism." It was a cold season of the year, and I suppose their vehemence give them heat, and from 9 o'clock in the morning till 5 o'clock at night, argued the question, with the result that each were still of the same opinion. Baxter satisfied his own people, and even some of Mr. Tomb's townsmen, but a number of Anabaptists refused to be convinced against their will. His disputes with the quakers in the Church, the Ranters, and other sectaries attempting settlement in the Town to their failure, marked him out to his townsmen, as a Minister of no mean order, in his riper years. To him all outside his line of religious thought were guilty of schism, and the making of these several sects in the Church most mischievous. To his writings, and also the presence, and support of honest justices of the peace, and bailiffs, as well other advantages claimed, his labours in the Town were such as to bind all in friendship, and in enjoyment of peace.

To the rule and authority of the Lord Protector, he gave but slight support, to Baxter he was the embodiment of all guilt, what said to his credit, best left unsaid. He acknowledges that from his privileged position in the pulpit, he did not dare to rave against him, nor unseasonably, and imprudently as might irritate him to mischief. When his lot would have been as those of other offenders. When the Commonwealth fell in 1659, the Presbyterians and Royalists combined to bring about the Restoration of K. Charles II. in 1660, and in the April of that year, being a day of humiliation, he preached before the Houses, and on that for thanksgiving at St. Paul's, before the Lord Mayor, hence it can be seen his aspirations were high. And after the arrival of the King, the 26th June, following appointed to office of Royal Chaplain. An office soon after made void, and a forerunner of the lot, he was to bear. The King in his declaration from Breda, said nothing about Church

Government, many of the Puritan Ministers thinking they would not be interfered with, but one of the first Acts of the Convention Parliament (12 Charles II.) was to restore, and confirm in office, those Ministers of the Anglican Church, ejected by former ordinances of the Parliamentary Committees, set up during the disruption. By which the hope of the Puritan Ministers were suspensory. Meanwhile the prelacy and presbyterians were seeking the superiority, and the hopes and fears of each, as it were, in the balance. The Bishoprics were early filled up, and Dr. George Morley made Bishop of Worcester on the 9th of October 1660. A conference was held in the Savoy (April 15—July 25, 1661), between 12 Bishops, and 12 leading Presbyterians

[Hallam's Hist. Vol. 2, p. 454 gives 21 on each side.]

in which Dr. Morley, and Richard Baxter, strongly disputed, for their respective sides. The main argument being that of the Presbyterian alterations in the Liturgy. There being no chance of agreement it was dissolved, more angry than ever. The Parliament elected in May 1661, utterly destroyed all Non-confirmists' hopes. The solemn Leage, and Covenant of 1644 (to extirpate Popery, to overthrow the established Church, to maintain sound doctrine, rights, and privileges of Parliament, the King's person and authority, preservation and defence of the true religion, and liberty of the subjects, etc.) and the declaration of the Commonwealth (1653) were ordered to be burnt by the common hangman, which was done before Baxter's door in the High Street, while he was dining with a few friends, having preached his last sermon the day before, the subject matter being on Christ's words on the cross, " Father, forgive them, for they know not what they do."

axter
377.

In the same session of Parliament, the Corporation Act was passed compelling all corporate officers to receive the sacrament, according to the rite of the Church of England, and to take the oath of non-resistance, to which

Baxter p.p. 376-377.

many of those non-conforming refused. Baxter tells that the 13 capital Burgesses, Bailiff and Justice of the Peace and all save one who had been a King's officer, and almost all the 25 Lower Burgesses, refusing, were turned out of office.

Baxter p.p. 298-299.

Baxter p. 301.

The old vicar, Mr. Dance came into his own again, and Sir Ralph Clare, in conjunction with the Bishop of Worcester, threw every impediment in Baxter's way. Clarendon offered him the Bishopric of Hereford, seeing the old vicar would not give way the price being Baxter's conformity. Hence Baxter was without a cure . . the Bishop refusing him licence, and coming to the Church to preach against him, and he so desirous to remain, begged to be allowed to preach the Gospel, without maintainance, and leave to beg his bread. In the following year (1662) 13 and 14 Car II. completely dissevered Baxter from his flock, and the Church of Kidderminster. This being the Act of Uniformity, and which came into operation, St. Bartholomew's day, August 24—1662. A notable day in the history of the Church. While these several incidents happened, the crown had appointed Lord Windsor, Lord Lieutenant of the Coy. of Worcester, having bought a house in the town, and lived amongst them, upon whom Baxter waited, and asked his intervention, in any strife, or misrepresentation, by anyone, against his old flock, whose sole desire was to live in peace with all men, for before his Lordship came, many were imprisoned, and harshly used. While debarred from his Ministry, and going in the town he on one occasion met Sir Ralph Clare with others searching the houses in the town for hidden arms. Meeting him soon after with the Bishop of Worcester, in the street, he desired to know the cause, as if the people were enemies to the King (Charles II.) It appears, an order was issued for all to deliver up the arms in their possession at a certain time and place, but none were found beyond such as were as a Byelaw, aforementioned (1640) allowed. Sir Ralph saying they always appeared to be armed in Cromwell's time, and to which Baxter replied with indignation, that it was untrue, and that he and the corporation had always spoken against Cromwell as a usurper, and much more to the like effect. Baxter still remaining in the town, and undecided how to act, his old friends fearing his stay, and their intercourse would be their ruin, he left them to the care of his former assistant, Mr. Thomas Baldwin. And although he and Sir Ralph Clare differed in their religious views, the old man must have admired his character, by his offering as a parting gift, a purse of gold, which Baxter refused to take. In the prime of his manhood, and a people to whom he had endeared himself, he went sorrowfully away, never more to return, but keeping up correspondence with some. Many of his old friends remained faithful to his teaching, meeting together secretly in out of the way places, and the records in the Bishop's Registry, Worcester, show in the after years, persons cited, and admonished " for not going to Church, pretended curates, brawling in Church, for slander, heretics to prove their marriage, excommunication, etc.," and whom the Toleration Act of William III. and Mary (1689) allowed to come into public view, and so originated that congregational body, known as Presbyterian, who in 1694 erected a Church for the worship, and service of God, on the back part of that now bearing his name, near to the Town Bridge, in Kidderminster.

The Lord Windsor mentioned is thus given in Collins's Peerage Vol. VI. Ed. 1779. Thomas Windsor Hickman Esqe was the son of Dixie Hickman, who married Elizabeth, eldest daughter, and co heir of Henry 5th Lord Windsor. By the death of his uncle Henry 6th Lord Windsor in 1642, who died without issue, he succeeded to all his possessions being a minor at that time, in ward of Lord Saye and Sele, the master of Wards, and Liveries. This Thomas, though but 15 years of age, brought to his Majesty, a good troop of horse, which at his own expense he maintained, and from time to time, recruited during the war, and behaving himself in several battles, and sharp encounters with valor, and loyalty, especially in that near Naseby, on June 14th 1645, where he stoutly charged with his regiment of horse, through, and through, the enemies army, and the King taking special notice thereof, ordered that he, and his regiment should be his royal guard for the day. But all being lost in the said fatal battle, and the King compelled to retreat to Ashby-de-la-Zouch, co Leicester, and acknowledging in particular, the merits of this Thomas Windsor, for his skill therein, and in special testimony, gave order for reviving the title, and dignity of Lord Windsor, to the said Thomas Windsor, but the matter lay in abeyance until the restoration of Charles II. who in consideration of his many good services throughout the war, as also his sufferings by imprisonment, plunder, and otherwise, did by patent June 16, 1660 restore him to the title, and dignity of Lord Windsor, and on July 18 following, constituted him Lord Lieutenant of Worc[r] in which office he remained until appointed Governor of Jamaica 1665. The Restoration period was one of confusion, requiring a strong hand, to control dissension, and out off chaos to make order. No doubt Lord Windsor knowing Kidderminster, to be an area most disaffected to the Royal cause, and the presence, and influence of Baxter, therein, was as equally determined on his removal, as the Inhibition of the Bishop, and so chose for a residence the Mansion house named in the parish, to restrain any rising, Baxter, no doubt waited upon him fearing retaliation for the sufferings his Lordship had undergone, and its visitation upon the party, of which Baxter himself was a member, to excite pity towards his friends, not conforming as required by Law, for qualification to temporal office.

Printed and Published by G. T. Cheshire & Sons, Kidderminster

JOHN BASKERVILE,

(1706-1775),

The Printer: His Ancestry.

RICHARD BAXTER,

(1615-1662),

: and Kidderminster. :

A Retrospect

by

THOMAS CAVE

(*Member Worcestershire Historical Society*).

3/6

1923.

PRINTED AND PUBLISHED BY G. T. CHESHIRE & SONS, KIDDERMINSTER.

ROWTON, SHROPSHIRE
The birthplace of Richard Baxter on Sunday 12 November 1615

Jennifer and I visited Rowton on Sunday 25th June 2000. It is a hamlet in the old English tradition, being situated at the end of a narrow lane off a main road to the north of Telford. There are houses, a few farms and a 19th century church. None of the buildings in Rowton are earlier than the 18th century and therefore after Baxter's time. However, on talking to a house owner, it is likely that some of the older houses were reconstructed from earlier settlements, as was the church. Although Baxter would not be immediately familiar with the Rowton of the 21st century, the contours of the land, the old road and perhaps even the antecedents of todays cottages would surely be recognizable. There is a monument at Rowton recording Baxter's connection with the hamlet. In the churchyard, I found one gravestone of a Baxter, a young man of 19 who died in the middle of the 19th century. The Parish register includes about two dozen names - none of them Baxter.

Rowton, Shropshire. Baxter's Monument

The wording on the stone

Rowton Church ~ Shropshire

Rowton Church ~ Showing gravestone of James Baxter who died 1865, the only reference to a Baxter name I was able to see

BRIDGNORTH, SHROPSHIRE

Baxter's house in Bridgnorth 1639-1641
opposite St. Leonard's Church.

Richard Baxter was the Curate to the Parish Church of St. Leonard in Bridgnorth during 1640 and 1641. Bridgnorth was taken by Parliamentary troops from the Royalists. St. Leonard's had the misfortune to have been converted into an ammunition store. Cannon shot from the castle caused a severe fire in the church and surrounding buildings, destroying the whole of High Town. The square is now beautifully restored, with Baxter's house positioned peacefully in the church square. A chapel stood next to St. Leonard's which was used as a Grammar School, subsequently rebuilt, as was St. Leonards after the Civil War.

Parish Church of St. Leonard Bridgnorth. Richard Baxter was Curate 1640-1641

The Richard Baxter Statue with St. Mary's Church, Kidderminster

St. Mary's Church, Kidderminster, with Richard Baxter Statue, foreground

The Baxter Chair,
St. Mary's Church, Kidderminster

The Baxter United Reform Church, Kidderminster foreground, showing St. Mary's in the Distance

The Baxter United Reform Church, Kidderminster

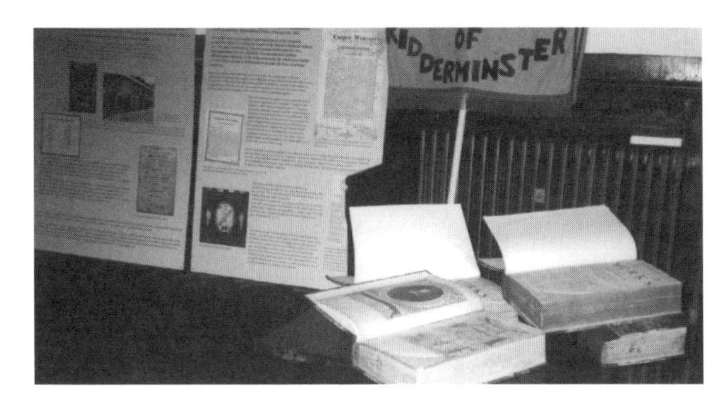

The collected works of Richard Baxter on display for public viewing at The New Meeting Church, Kidderminster

New Meeting Church, Kidderminster

The Baxter Pulpit which dates from 1621. It was bought by the founder of New Meeting Church, Nicholas Pearsall in about 1785 and came from St. Mary's.

IMPORTANT DATES AND EVENTS AROUND BAXTER'S TIME

DATE	EVENT
1606	First Charter of Virginia
1608	Rubens painting at Antwerp
1609	Scientific discoveries of Gallileo
1610	Henry Hudson discovers Hudson Bay
1612	Opening of first London Theatre
1614	Dutch settlers to New Amsterdam, (fur traders)
1618	Beginning of 30 years War (Catholic Holy Roman Emperor versus German Protestant States, later involving France, Sweden, Spain. Most fighting was in Germany. Bourbon France became dominant European power.)
1622	Start of Richelieu's permanent ministry, France
1625	Huguenot revolt in France
1628	Building of Taj Mahal
1633	Inquisition forces Galileo to recant
1634	Milton's "Comus" was acted in Ludlow (Baxter was at Court in Ludlow - were "Comus" and the Shakespeare plays the ones which caused Baxter to be repelled by so called, lewd displays and immoral nature?)
1636	Foundation of Harvard University
	Dutch conquest of Ceylon
1639	English factory set up in Madras
1642	Birth of Isaac Newton
1647	Accession of William II of Orange in Holland
1648	George Fox founds the Quakers
1649	Maryland ordains religious toleration
1650	Death of William II of Orange
1652	Dutch settle Cape of Good Hope
1654	Petty's survey of Ireland
1655	Charles X of Sweden attacks Poland
1659	Pepys begins his diary
1662	Building of Versailles
1664	Defeat of Turks at St. Golthard
1665	The London Gazette founded
1666	Newton discovers gravity law
1667	Milton's "Paradise Lost"
1669	Fall of Crete to Turks
	Death of Rembrandt
1670	Locke drafts a Constitution for Carolina

1673	Hapsburgs help Dutch resist French
1675	Prussian victory over Swedes
1677	Publication of Spinoza's "Ethics" and his death.
1681	Founding of Pennsylvania French seize Strasbourg
1684	Locke expelled from Oxford
1686	League of Augsberg (Bavaria) against France. Also in 1530, was the Augsberg Confession, a Lutheran statement presented to Emperor Charles V. Buda Pesth taken from Turks
1687	Venetians destroy Parthenon Newton "Principia"
1688	France declares war on Holland
1689	Locke "Civil Government"
1690	English settlement in Calcutta
1691	Turks lose Transylvania
1692	Lloyds begin marine insurance
1693	Halley's observation of transit of Venus

WITCHCRAFT

I referred to 'Universal Encyclopedia' 1928 for the following analysis of witchcraft and its appalling impact. Baxter believed there were such people as witches and denounced them throughout his life. All the power of the law and the church were used to prosecute the case against the accused, almost always a woman.

It is estimated that between 1484 and 1782 in Europe that 300,000 witches suffered death. Such persons were occasionally lynched, often burnt. The term applied to sorcery or magic alledged to be practised by women in league with demons. Witches were believed to cause death or injury by spells and potions, to raise storms and blast crops and cattle .... to gain wealth, gratify lust, to know future events, travel through the air on broomsticks and be able to transform into animals.

From 1258, witchcraft was treated as heresy by the INQUISITION, in which there was a fanatical fear of an anti-Christian conspiracy. (Was this linked to fear of the Muslim religion? Were witches accused of being Muslim ever?)

In 1434, Pope Innocent VIII issued a Proclamation, quoting Bible Texts - Ex.XXII, 18 provided a ground for execution by burning.

The high Churches of the Christian Religion, Catholic and Protestant, prosecuted the anti-witch philosophy. Confessions were gained under torture. Obviously not all people were actively Christian. Paganism was still apparent. Those Pagans, particularly women, were likely candidates for burning.

Most witches may have been normal, others hysterical or insane, still others may have been condemned through suggestion and physical phenomena.
Persecution of witches spread to America and so the New Beginning took with it the fear and violent reprisal against those accused. In Salem in 1692,the whole town fell victim to anti-witchcraft hysteria. Men and women were accused and killed, with their children.
British penal laws concerning Witchcraft were only repealed in 1736, forty five years after Baxter's death. The last execution for Witchcraft in Britain took place at Dornoch in 1722.

THE 'BLACK DEATH'

In 14th century Europe, the Black Death killed one quarter of the population. Disease was indicated by "Plague Spots" of blood haemorrhages. Plague was a disease of rats, infected by rat fleas which bit rats and humans. In the Great Plague of London 1665-1666, some 70,000-100,000 people perished.

THE GREAT FIRE OF LONDON

1666 Two thirds of the area within London's City Walls was reduced to ashes by the fire. Baxter witnessed the Great Fire of London.

RELIGIOUS LEADERS AND MOVEMENTS, LITERARY AND POLITICAL FIGURES

MARTIN LUTHER 1483 -1546

German reformer. University of Erfurt, entered Erfurt monastery as a Monk. Evangelical attitude, 1508 to University of Wittenberg, taught and preached.

Affronted by John Tetzel selling Papal Indulgences. Luther questioned Forgiveness of Sins in public. According to usual academic form, posted up certain of these for discussion.

Luther's 95 Theses were thunderbolts, 1517 - began REFORMATION which shook Christendom. Luther was summond to Rome, but conferences were arranged instead, and order withdrawn. Church conference Leipzig 1519. Conference did not convert Luther, but made him a popular hero, asserting truth and freedom against Papal corruption.

Treatise on Christian Liberty; The Reformation of the Christian Estate, The Babylonish Captivity of the church. 1520 - Papel Bull condemned Luther. He burned it publicly in Wittenberg. Summond tothe Diet at Worms 1521.

Luther's journey was a royal progress - he would not retreat. "Here I stand, I can do no other." Left Worms 1522 under warning, to castle at Wartburg. Wrote German translation of the Bible and many hymns.

Peasant War - Luther urged Princes to put it down thereby losing popular sympathy for Protestant cause.

1525 - Luther married Catherine Von Bora who had been a Nun - this caused scandal.

NOTES ON LUTHERANISM

The Pope excommunicated Luther.
1525 -27 Luther appointed superintendent to co-ordinate his Evangelical Church with secular authorities. The Government of the church consistories, worked with territorial princes,controlled and administered to poor and schools. Not democratic, unlike Calvin churches.

JOHN CALVIN 1509 -64 (FRENCH)

French Protestant Theologian. Paris University 1523.
Law School at Orleans, wrote book on Seneca's, "De Clementia" 1532.
1529 - conversion to Protestantism. 1533, avowed Protestant, returned to Paris, but

had to leave under pressure.
1535 to Basel. Wrote Treatise, "Christian Religion" 1536
To Geneva 1536, Geneva supported REFORMATION, and was in revolt against ROME.
Calvin set up a NEW MORAL CODE. GENEVA expelled CALVIN and FARREL.1538 CALVIN to STRASBOURG, TO STUDY and lectured to all EVANGELICAL churches.
Contact with GERMAN REFORMATION, he married Ideletta de Bure (died 1549)
1541, Recalled to GENEVA, declared Geneva, "City of God" Calvin considered religion for community and the individual. His system was very ECCLESIASTICAL and evoked jealousy.
CALVIN used penalties of the state to enforce spiritual and moral discipline.
He reduced the poverty of GENEVA, improved its health and founded GENEVA UNIVERSITY.
CALVIN gave PROTESTANTISM an organised system of DOCTRINE and POLITY

JOHN KNOX 1515-1572

Educated St. Andrew's University. Took minor orders, in 1540 was apostolical notary at Haddington. Knox befriended Wishart the Martyr who preached at East Lothian 1545.
Knox embraced the Reformed faith.
Wishart's persecutor, Cardinal Beaton, was murdered, Knox fled to St.Andrew's Castle, which was held by the murderers. Knox became garrison preacher.
The castle surrendered to the French 1547. Knox consigned to French galleys, released 1549, after English Government interceded.
Knox played notable part in Reformation under Edward V1 as a preacher in Berwick and Newcastle as a Royal Chaplain, and as inspirer of the "Black Rubric", retained in the Prayer book to explain significance of Kneeling at C ommunion.
On Mary Tudor's accession he visited Switzerland on CALVIN'S ADVICE became MINISTER to English refugees at FRANKFURT, November 1554.
Left FRANKFURT over PRAYER book disputes 1555. Chosen by ENGLISH EXILES as PASTOR in GENEVA 1556 - CALVINS City of God"
He visited Scotland, gave vigour to Protestants returned Geneva 1566. Stayed two and a half years.
Enjoyed " Rule of Saints" Reached Dieppe. returned Scotland 1559.
Protestant Nobles were in arms against the Regent, Mary of Guise. KNOX supported this cause.
1560. French troops left Scotland.
PAPAL authority was ABOLISHED, replaced by CALVINISTIC "Confession of

Faith," drawn up by Knox. Nobles prevented ratification of FIRST Book of Discipline - gaining revenues of old church for the new and promotion of Calvin's ideals - religious,social, moral and intellectual. For the well being of people, Mary returned to Scotland, she was allowed MASS. It was assumed she would change her religion to inherit the English throne, but she did not.
Knox denounced her from PULPIT in St. Giles Church.
Interviews with Mary by Knox.
Mary abdicated. MORAY was appointed Regent.
Knox was recognised as Protestant church leader by Parliament, Moray was appointed Regent under the 1567 + 1560 Acts in favour of PROTESTANTISM.
1570 CIVIL WAR followed, MORAY assasinated. Knox opposed Queen Mary, held Edinburgh Castle then he withdrew to St, Andrew's MAY 1571. "Half dead". Returned to Edinburgh Aug.1572 preached last sermon at St. Giles.

WILLIAM SHAKESPEARE

Baptised 26th April 1564, died 23rdApril 1616.
Married Ann Hathaway 1582, his senior by eight years.
Daughter Susanna, born 1583 and twins Hamnet and Judith 1585 [son died at 12 yrs.]
1587 - to London employed at The Theatre [later Globe] Shoreditch, the only playhouse existing. Admitted to company of actors - patrons to theatre were Elizabeth's favourite Earl of Leicester then, James I. James licensed Shakespear's company 1603-became "The Kings Servants." Performed at Royal Palaces.
Shakespeare played in Ben Johnsons Comedy. "Every Man in his Humour.' 1598

1591-1611

Shakespeare's dramatic work [Shared " Pericles" etc. with others]
Collections of Shakespeare's work were published throughout the next 80 years [during Baxters time] up until 1709 [edited version by Rowe] 4th folio, 1685.

THOMAS HOBBES

Born at Malmessbury 1588, died 1679. Contemporary of Bacon and Ben Johnsson, instructor to Prince Charles. Mathematician, physics, rationalism and politics. Left for France in 1640, associated with Gassendi and French intellectuals. His materialism offended churchmen from among the English expatriates. 1651 returned to England. Wrote "De Cive" :1642,
"Leviathan" 1651, "De Corpore Politico" 1650, "De Homine" 1658, "Behemoth" 1680.

Leviathan was Hobbes development of his political philosophy and the mechanical interpretation of human activity and progress. Hobbes was the first great political theorist. .

JOHN MILTON 1608 - 1674

English Poet and prose writer. Born Cheapside 9th December, 1608

His father was a scrivener, and a Puritan, a lover also of literature and music. The child enjoyed a cultivated home. St. Pauls School and Christ's College Cambridge. Retired to his father's house for studying, 1632 - 1638. He wrote "L'Allegro" and "Il Penseroso" 1633, the masque "Comus" 1634, "LyCidas" 1637, an elegy on the death of his college friend, Edward King, in which he openly proclaimed his Puritanism.

1638 May - abroad, the continent, to Naples, where Milton heard of English civil unrest, "my fellow citizens were fighting for liberty," He abandoned his tour in Greece, returned to England.

1638 - 1658, Milton devoted these years to Politics and Prose.
1643 - 1645 wrote, "Doctrine and Discipline of Divorce."
1644 "Tractate on Education."
1644 Tract on Liberty of the Press, "Areopagitica".
1649 -1650 After execution of Charles 1st, " Tenure of Kings and Magistrates"- Milton was seen as most eloquent exponent of New Regime. Appointed Latin secretary to Foreign Affairs Committee.
1649 - Milton acted as publicist for Cromwell's Government - "Eikonoklastes,"
1651 - "Defensio pro Populo Anglicano" & "Defensio Secunda" 1654, during which he became totally BLIND.
1643 - married Mary Powell, died 1653.
1656 - married Catherine Woodcock, died 1658.
1660 - Restoration - left Milton impoverished.
1667 - "Paradise Lost," ..."the epic of a lost cause".
1670 - "History of Britain"
1673 - "Theatre of True Religion"
1663 - third wife - Elizabeth Minshull. Milton - was a child of the Renaissance, his avowed pupose was, "to justify the ways of God to men."

JOHN LOCKE 1632 - 1704

English philosopher. His father was a lawyer who had served in the Parliamentary army. Locke attended Westminster School and Christ Church, Oxford, where he became a tutor, then Private Secretary to Earl of Shaftesbury, with whose political career he was associated for 15 years. Board of Trade Secretary for 3 years.

1675 - 1679 Locke was in France
1683 - Locke to Holland, known to William of Orange.
1689 - returned to England, began career as an author.
1690 - Essay on Human Understanding, additions in 1700, "Association of Ideas." Locke is the originator of materialism and empiricism. He denies the existence of innate ideas, asserts that the source of all knowledge is experience. As a political philosopher, Locke enunciated the Whig theory of Government. His ideas are contained in Two Treatise on Government, stating the case for sovereignty of the people, the basis of democratic government. His "Letters on Toleration" are arguments for liberty of thought. His first work appeared anonymously in 1689, written in Latin. "Thoughts on Education" 1693, "The Reasonableness of Christianity", caused controversy. Locke wrote also on monetary subjects.

SAMUEL PEPYS 1633 - 1703

English diarist and admiralty official

Imprisoned in Tower 1679 and Gatehouse, Westminster 1690.
Member of Parliament for Harwich.
His diary 1st January 1659 - 31st May 1669

JOHN BUNYAN 1628 - 1688

English author and Preacher. Worked at his fathers trade, a tinker , took part in Civil War during 1644 - 45 probably serving in Parliamentary army.
Married 1648, wife's dowry, 2 books "The Plain Man's Pathway to Heaven" and "The Practice of Piety", Reading led to later religious conversion with Puritan fervour, he abandoned dancing and bell ringing.
Bunyan became a Nonconformist Preacher 1657. 1660 convicted for unauthorised preaching.
Spent 12 years in Bedford gaol. Wrote 1666 - "Grace abounding to the Chief of Sinners.'
1672 Declaration of Indulgence - Bunyan released
1675 Prison again. Began to write 'Pilgrim's Progress' Part 1 published 1678, part 2 in 1684, 100,000 copies sold in 10 years.

JUDGE JEFFREYS

George Jeffreys 1st Baron, lived 1648 - 1689.
Born Denbighshire.
Educated St. Pauls and Westminster schools and Trinity College, Cambridge
Called to the BAR 1668
REPUTATION - forcible speech and hectoring manner.

1678 - Recorder of city of London.
Persecuted those involved in POPISH PLOT, April 24th 1678.
An ex-Jesuit, Titus Oates, declared Jesuit Congregation of England had met at White Horse Tavern, London and had planned overthrow of Charles II and installation of Catholicism. The story was a lie, but brought a reign of TERROR and execution of CATHOLICS.
1683, JUDGE JEFFREYS was made Chief Justice of Kings Bench.
1684 - Jeffreys tried RICHARD BAXTER - sentenced him to prison June 1685 til Nov.1686.
1685 - Jeffreys was made a BARON.
1685 - MONMOUTH REBELLION - the Trial was conducted brutally by Jeffreys. Leaders and others were executed; followers transported to West Indies.
1685 - Jeffreys became LORD CHANCELLOR in September, whereupon he tried to secure "unconstitutional claims," of JAMES II
In the "BLOODLESS REVOLUTION" OF 1688, Jeffreys was arrested on12th December and died a PRISONER in the TOWER OF LONDON, 18th April 1689.

HENRY PURCELL 1658 - 1695

English Composer, born London. Organist Westminster Abbey 1680 and organist, Chapel Royal 1682.
1675 - first Opera, "Dido and Aeneas".
Composed many works for stage, 'Diocletian', 'King Arthur,'
'The Fairy Queen.'
Wrote church music, anthems, songs and odes.
Sonatas for strings and harpsichord.

SIR ISAAC NEWTON 1642 - 1727

Born 25th December 1642 Woolsthorpe, Lincolnshire.
Educated Grantham School & Trinity College, Cambridge.
1665 At Trinity studying Euclidean Geometry, optics and chemistry.
1665 outbreak of Plague.
1666 His theory of Gravity.
1668 Elected Cambridge Fellow - lived for next 30 years in College. Elected Lucasian Professor.
1675 Crown issued letters - patent permitting him to hold his Fellowship without taking orders.
1696 Newton left Cambridge for London. Held office in the Mint.
Newton was a deeply religious man.

NOTES ON THE ANABAPTISTS

The meaning of Anabaptist is to Baptise again.
Anabaptists were a fanatical Protestant sect under Thomas Munzer in 1520.
They rejected INFANT BAPTISM.
Required BAPTISM in later life.
Anabaptists held that existing order should be destroyed and replaced by a new DIVINE order
Anabaptists advocated doing away with all inequalities and private property.
They also advocated polygamy.
Munzer's doctrine inspired the GERMAN PEASANTS REVOLT in 1625.
MUNZER was put to death.
According to Universal Encyclopedia 1928, throughout the 16th century, the term Anabaptist was used for all PROTESTANTS whose doctrines appeared to be subversive of ecclesiastical and political order.
After 1535 and the execution of John of Leiden, the Anabaptists, as an actual sect, disappeared.

BAPTISTS

Baptists constitute one branch of Evangelical Protestants.
JOHN SMYTH an English Clergyman became a separatist, a Pastor of Gainsborough church.
He fled to Amsterdam 1608.
1609 - he abandoned INFANT BAPTISM "Baptism intended for believers only."
In Amsterdam, the English refugees formed the first BAPTIST CHURCH in 1611.
Thomas Helwys, a follower , returned to England in 1612, and formed First BAPTIST CHURCH practising believers Baptism - the immersion of believer in water.
1st Church - Newgate Street London.
"A PLEA FOR LIBERTY of CONSCIENCE" was addressed to, SMYTH 1611, then Leonard Busher in 1614 - and to KING JAMES Ist.
During the COMMONWEALTH - BAPTISTS prospered. Many of Cromwells Ironsides and Officers were BAPTISTS who became PREACHERS and FOUNDERS of CHURCHES.
There were General and Particular Baptists. The General Baptists held their first General Assembly in 1654. The Particular Baptists formed associations to pursue their creed.

AFTER THE RESTORATION OF 1660

Baptists were persecuted, but their cause advanced, Particular Baptists Churches held a London Assembly at which over one hundred churches were represented.

PURITANS

Were Protestants of the 16th century who wished to "purify" the Church of England from superstitious and corrupt observances retained after the severance from Rome. The doctrine was Calvanistic.The Stuarts were repressive towards PURITANISM, so Parliamentary opposition to the Crown focused upon the Puritans, who claimed to be champions of RELIGIOUS LIBERTY.
The leading Puritans- MILTON, CROMWELL and BUNYAN.
STUART RESTORATION 1660 - PURITANS ousted.
NEW ENGLAND States were a PURITAN stronghold.

COVENANTERS

Those who signed the "National League and Covenant" to acknowledge no other head of the Church than Jesus Christ.
Baxter was offered any position in Scotland, by Earl of Lauderdale, his friend, but declined.

QUAKERS - SOCIETY OF FRIENDS

Began in middle of 17th century, as a revolt of mystical or spiritual Christianity against the ecclesiasticism and bibliolatry of the Reformed Churches, both Anglican and Nonconformist. George Fox was a first disciple and leader. He received no help from the established church, but believed God had spoken to him directly, as to the ancient prophets
Followers gathered as, "Children of the Light," many became preachers travelling throughout Britain, the Continent and American Colonies. Early advocates were Penington,Penn, Ellwood and Barclay.
The objective was not to create a new religious sect, but to return the Christian Church, "back from the dark into the light of truth."
For over 70 years, Penn's Quakers in Pennsylvania Colony ruled without armed defence against Indian attack, nor indeed were they attacked.

QUAKERS Continued

After the Toleration Act of 1689 persecution for the most part ceased, "a time of mystiacal Quietism and decline set in."
Quaker practices flow from the principle of "inner light," individuals can have direct experience of God in the soul
In public worship Quakers discard all professional ministry and arranged services and meet in silent fellowship and waiting on God, giving freedom to any man or woman who is selected to be moved by the Spirit to preach or lead the company in vocal prayer.
Quakers do not practice Baptism and the Lords Supper- the symbolic acts; believing Christ's emphasis was on inward experience and rightness of life.
Quakers refuse to take judicial oaths, and have unique form of marriage; The man and woman accept one another in the presence of God and Congregation.
In church government, every man or woman has an equal voice. No question is decided by a vote. The clerk gathers the sense of the meeting, decisions are rarely challenged,
In America Quakers were first to forbid its members to hold slaves.

PRESBYTERIANISM

Is the name for the organisation of the Christian Church on the basis of rule by presbyters.
These are chosen by the congregations, they teach and rule.
Presbyters are equal in rank,elect temporary moderators - have synods and general assemblies.
Presbyters are ordained for life, as ministers or elders.
From the 17th century onwards a hot controversy raged upon the divine right of episcopacy, church government by bishops.

PILGRIM FATHERS

Term applies to ENGLISH founders of PLYMOUTH COLONY, Massachusetts in 1620, from the church founded by John Robinson at Leiden, Holland after leaving England because of intolerance.
They obtained a grant of land from the Virginia Company in New Jersey, and a promise from the King James Ist, 2nd July of their freedom to worship.
They set sail from Plymouth in the The Mayflower, on 6th September 1620. They numbered seventy eight men and twenty four women.
Bad weather forced them to land on the coast of Massachusettes, far South of territory granted to them.

Here they founded Plymouth Colony.
Massachusetts Bay Colony was founded by English PURITANS 1629-30.
Massachusetts Bay Colony and Plymouth Colony were united in 1691.
(James 1st. 1603-1625)

BILL OF RIGHTS 1689

The Convention Parliament met after the flight of James II in 1688 and offered the Crown to William and Mary.
The terms of that offer were incorporated in the Declaration of Rights, an affirmation of all principles fought for by Parliament for 60 years.
The Bill a] declares the RIGHTS AND LIBERTIES of SUBJECTS.
b]settles the SUCCESSION of the CROWN.
Bill/ACT - declares many/all JAMES II ACTS to be UNCONSTITUTIONAL.
AND - declares JAMES II ABDICATED, thereby the Throne was vacant,
and - a CONVENTION PARLIAMENT had been called.
Held that Laws could not be suspended, Crown needed Parliament to raise money; subjects may Petition King; Keeping a standing army needed Parliament's consent; election of Members to Parliament should be free; Freedom of speech; Against excessive fines and bails; Frequent Parliaments enshrined.

BILL OF RIGHTS Contiued

Provided settlement on William & Mary, declared King and Queen of England, France & Ireland.
William was to have sole Regal power.
If they left no children, the Crown would pass to PRINCESS ANNE and her issue.
Oaths OF ALLEGIANCE and SUPREMACY - the latter declared vigorously against THE POPE.
LATER CLAUSE - NO ROMAN CATHOLIC nor one married to a R.C. should inherit crown.

BIBLIOGRAPHY

"THE SAINT'S EVERLASTING REST," Richard Baxter. 1650. Edited with an introduction by John T. Wilkinson. Published in 1962 by the Epworth Press, Camelot Ltd. London.

"RICHARD BAXTER, The Saints Everlasting Rest and The Mayor's Parlour in Kidderminster." Compiled and Published by Cllr. Mike Oborski 1995 with articles by Don Gilbert, Chairman of the Richard Baxter Society.

"RICHARD BAXTER 1615-1691", W.Stuart Owen. 1981.
Published by Owen Publications. Beale House, Blakebrook, Kidderminster.

"BEWDLEY PARISH MAGAZINES 1878 & 1880." Nigel Knowles 1999.
Published by Star & Garter Publishers, 18 Welch Gate, Bewdley.
In the "Bewdley Parish Magazine 1878" there is an account under "Bewdley Worthies" of the Reverend Henry Oasland M.A. a contemporary and friend of Richard Baxter. Together they preached, "ye Double Lecture in ye County."

"A PEOPLES HISTORY OF ENGLAND," A.L.Morton 1976
Published by Lawrence & Wishart Ltd. London.

"BRITISH POPULATION GROWTH 1700-1850," M.W.Finn 1970
Published by the MacMillan Press Ltd. London.

The book gives good account of population in Britain, with references to 17th, 18th and 19th centuries, citing economic and social explanations for increase. Population in 1695 was 5.2 million.

"THE ENGLISH REVOLUTION 1640," Christopher Hill.
Lawrence & Wishart Ltd. 1940 & 1979. Camelot Ltd. Southampton.

"THE DECLINE OF SERFDOM in Medieval England,"
R.H.Hilton 1969. Published by MacMillan Ltd London.

"ANNALS OF THE POOR," Eve McLoughlin. 1979
Published by Varneys Press, Haddenham, Aylesbury.

"ECONOMIC HISTORY OF ENGLAND," Briggs & Jordan. Twelfth edition 1967. Published by University Tutorial Press Ltd. London.

"THE EVELYNS IN AMERICA 1608-1805," G.D.Scull 1881. Printed by Parker & Co. Oxford, 250 copies, for private circulation.
Some of the early settlers in America read Baxter's work.
Book gives graphic original detail of life in 17th century.

"ENGLISH ECONOMIC HISTORY" J.S.Dugdale 1961.
Published by James Brodie Ltd. London

"FREEDOM IN ARMS - a selection of Leveller Writings."
A.L.Morton. Published by Lawrence & Wishart London. 1975

"THE CIVIL WAR IN WORCESTERSHIRE 1642 - 1646 and The Scotch Invasion of 1651." J.W. Willis Bund Birmingham. The Midland Education Company Ltd [1905].

"THE CARPET WEAVERS OF KIDDERMINSTER." Arther Marsh 1995.
Published by Malthouse Press, Oxford.
Gives brief account of early carpet manufacture. References to "Kidderminster Stuff" - material used for wall hangings, upholstery and bed coverings. The Borough had produced woollen stuffs since the 13th century. Marsh lists also - broadcloths, worsted materials, cheyneys, rateens, poplin s, tammys & prunellas.

'Kidderminster Stuff,' was sold in 1660 at 1 shilling & 2 pence a yard [Linsey Woolsey]; heavier material at 5 shillings. The hand-loom method of weaving was finally superceded by the power-loom carpet industry in the 19th century.

"A HISTORY OF KING CHARLES 1ST. Grammar School Kidderminster,"
C.D. Gilbert 1980. Published by Kenneth Tomkinson Ltd. High Habberley House, Kidderminster.
This book gives an excellent history of the school in Baxter's time, with many valuable references to Baxter.

"KIDDERMINSTER SINCE 1800," Ken Tomkinson & George Hall. Published by the Authors 1975.
The excellent Book gives some pre-1800 history of the area. In 1608, the population of Kidderminster was 1500, in 1647 it was 2,200 in 1685 population was 3,000.
'Kidderminster stuffs' were floor coverings, as well as wall hangings

"BEWDLEY A 15TH CENTURY SANCTUARY TOWN," Jean Marsh 1979.
Published by Halmer, Kinver.
Like all authors, Miss Marsh has used many sources for her work. Bewdley is situated 3 miles from Kidderminster and is as old. It is interesting to consider the history of the two towns, to give comparison, one to the other. The Bewdley Woollen Cap industry was very important. An act of 1571 decreed all persons over seven years of age should wear English caps under forfeiture of three farthings for every days neglect. Bewdley employed over 1,000 people in this industry alone during the period.

A full list of Bewdley industries may be found in-

"BEWDLEY 1762 - THE DIARY OF JACK NOWLES," Nigel Knowles 1996,. Published by, Star and Garter Publishers.

"BEWDLEY IN ITS GOLDEN AGE," Bewdley Historical Research Group, 1991. Excellent account of life in the Bewdley area during Baxter's time.

"CALDWELL HALL KIDDERMINSTER," Don Gilbert and Richard Warner. Published by Kidderminster and District Aechoelogical and Historical Society 1999.
Home of Sir Ralph Clare a Royalist, to whom Baxter was opposed.

"ECHOES OF CANNON FIRE - A Malvern Hills View of the Civil War," Jeremy Webb 1995. Published by Jeremy Webb & Printed First Paige, Malvern. The book gives a nice account of Civil War activities in Malvern, Worcestershire and the surrounding Counties.

"A HISTORY OF ENGLAND," Sir Keith Feiling. Oxford 1948, Book Club.

ACKNOWLEDGEMENTS
AND
THANKS

The Reverend Canon D.Owain Bell, M.A., St. Mary's and All Saints, Kidderminster Parish Church. For his help, advice and friendship particularly during my time as Town Mayor of Kidderminster, when Owain kindly agreed to be my Chaplain.
Professor Trevor Haywood [of Kidderminster] for the loan of the Thomas Cave book of 1923, "Baskerville and Baxter" before I was fortunate to purchase my own copy from Lion Books of Bewdley on 13th May 2000.
To Don Gilbert for our chat on the telephone, and then later, for volunteering to read through the manuscript, offering genuine help, advice and correcting mistakes. My thanks to Don for our discussion over coffee in the Mayor's Parlour on Monday 23rd October 2000.
Roger Mathews, Edna Church and Elaine McRorie of The New Meeting Church, Kidderminster for their help and permission to take photographs of the Baxter Pulpit and his collected works.
George Hall and his wife, for the chat in their home and kind offer of tea.
Terry Salters, Lee Cordery and staff at Stargold Printers. (01562) 741603.